The Age of A Artificial Intelligence is Reshaping the World

Jason Mallory

Introduction

Technology has radically transformed daily life in recent decades. Those who lived in the 90s remember bulky computers, rudimentary cell phones and very slow internet connections, while today we live surrounded by powerful and always connected devices. This essay popularly explores the evolution of technology from the 1990s era to today, analyzing the key differences between the hardware and software then and now. Furthermore, we will review the progress of**artificial intelligence (AI)** and its impact on contemporary society, to then discuss possible future scenarios and the role that AI could have in the future of humanity. The text is organized into thematic chapters - from the technological comparison between yesterday and today, to the advantages and critical issues of AI in areas such as economy, privacy, work and human rights - supporting the arguments with academic sources, newspaper articles and official documents.

Over the last 30 years, we have gone from a world where the internet was a luxury for the few to a reality where more than half the world's population is online en.wikipedia.org
. In the 1990s, cell phones were expensive bricks with monochrome screens
mazumamobile.com
, while today **smartphone** pocket phones make extraordinary computing capabilities available to anyone -

just think of what a modern smartphone is about **5,000 times faster** of a Cray-2 supercomputer from the 1980s blog.adobe.com

. Likewise, theIA it has gone from being a field of experimental research to a widespread, if often invisible, presence in our everyday lives. Almost everyone uses AI-based services (search engines, social media, voice assistants, etc.) on a daily basis, often without realizing it news.gallup.com

. This widespread penetration of technology raises enthusiasm for the opportunities offered, but also questions and fears regarding the effects on the economy, work, privacy and fundamental rights.

In the following sections we will first analyze the characteristics of technology in the 90s compared to today, then we will retrace the stages of technological evolution and artificial intelligence. Subsequently we will discuss how AI affects daily life and we will delve into the benefits and critical issues of AI in the economic, work, privacy and human rights fields. Finally, we will reflect on future prospects and the role that AI could play in the destiny of humanity.

Chapter 1: Technology in the 90s

In the 1990s, digital technology took its first steps towards mass use. Personal computers were now common in offices and homes, but their capabilities were limited by today's standards. From the point of view **hardware**, a typical PC from the early 1990s might have an Intel 386 or 486 family processor and a few megabytes of RAM. For example, one user recalls starting with an IBM XT (derived from the original IBM PC) equipped with just **640 KB of memory** and a hard disk from **20 MB** healthdatamanagement.com

– features that are ridiculous today, thousands of times inferior to those of any smartphone. At the time, even a small upgrade was revolutionary: moving to a larger IDE hard drive was seen as a technological marvel healthdatamanagement.com

. Memory media was expensive and limited in capacity: in the 1990s a 40 MB hard disk could cost 240 dollars, while today a 32 GB USB stick (800 times the capacity) costs a few euros healthdatamanagement.com

. Many experts thought that there were

insurmountable limits to the power of computers. The words of a technician at the time are emblematic: *"they told us that computers could not exceed the speed of about 175 MHz because it would interfere with radio stations"* healthdatamanagement.com . Of course, these predictions turned out to be wrong, and the theoretical limits were exceeded by several orders of magnitude in the following years.

Also the **software** and operating systems in the 1990s were very different from those today. Most PCs still booted MS-DOS or early versions of Windows such as Windows 3.1; only in the middle of the decade did Windows 95 arrive with a friendlier graphical interface. Installing programs or operating systems required patience and physical media: the first version of Windows 95 was distributed on **21 floppy disk** 3.5 inch healthdatamanagement.com . It was a pre-broadband era: if today we download software from the Internet in a few minutes, at the time we inserted piles of diskettes. An article reminds us that to contain Windows 10 on floppy disks, you would need a lot of them **2.778**

healthdatamanagement.com
, a joking comparison that highlights how much the size of the software and the available memory capacity have increased. Video games and programs were also limited by hardware power: graphics were rudimentary, often 2D or with simple polygons, and user interfaces were less intuitive than today.

On the front of **telecommunications**, the 1990s saw the dawn of the internet and mobile phones, albeit in very immature forms compared to today. Mobile phones were huge and expensive: a "typical" cell phone in the early 1990s served almost exclusively for calls and texts, with tiny, monochrome screens.
mazumamobile.com
. Only towards the end of the decade did the first more compact GSM phones appear and text messaging services (SMS) became popular. The Internet, for its part, was new to a few enthusiasts and to the academic world. The connection was made via analogue dial-up modems, which emitted the famous sequence of crackling sounds during line negotiation. The initial velocity was **2400 baud**

(approximately 2.4 Kbps); at the end of the decade, with modems a **56k**, you could browse at a theoretical ~56 Kbps
healthdatamanagement.com
. It was slow and often expensive navigation (you paid by the time on telephone lines), suitable only for texts and small images. This is also why the use of the Internet was restricted: in **1996 there were about 45 million** of internet users around the world; at the end of 1999 they had risen to 150 million
elon.edu
, or only about 4% of the population at the time. Most of these early adopters were in the United States and Western Europe.

In summary, the technology in the 90s, although revolutionary for the time, appears "primitive" today. Underpowered computers, basic phones, and slow connections were the norm. Yet, it was in those years that the foundations were laid: the PC became a common object, the mobile phone began to spread and above all the Internet began its **"meteoritic growth"**
melita.com

. The 1990s gave us the World Wide Web (invented in 1989-90 by Tim Berners-Lee), the first browsers like Mosaic and Netscape healthdatamanagement.com

, pioneering search engines like AltaVista healthdatamanagement.com

, and services such as **America Online (AOL)** who sent CD-ROMs to people's homes to invite them to connect to the internet healthdatamanagement.com

. It was the beginning of a digital revolution, the extent of which few understood at the time.

Chapter 2: Today's technology

Today, 30 years later, the technological scenario has completely changed. We live in a world **hyperconnected** in which computing power and access to information are widely available to a large part of the world's population. From the point of view **hardware**, current devices are orders of magnitude more powerful and at the same time more compact. A common smartphone today packs billions of transistors into a few square centimeters of silicon and has multi-gigabytes of memory. As already mentioned, one **modern smartphone exceeds by thousands of times** the computational performance of computers from the 1990s: it is even thousands of times more powerful than a supercomputer from the early 1980s

blog.adobe.com

. This was possible thanks to the continuous progress described by **Moore's law**, formulated by Gordon Moore, co-founder of Intel, according to which the number of transistors in integrated circuits doubles approximately every two years (originally Moore spoke of an annual doubling)

while the cost per single transistor halves
blog.adobe.com
. For decades this trend has continued, making computers increasingly faster and cheaper. Although Moore's pace has begun to slow in recent years, the cumulative impact is immense: what in the 1990s required a dedicated machine costing tens of thousands of euros can now be done with a phone costing a few hundred euros.

In addition to advances in raw power, there has been a huge evolution in **types of devices**. In the 90s the digital device par excellence was the fixed PC (desktop) or at most the **laptop** (notebook), which however was expensive and less common. Today we have a variety of devices: **smartphone, tablet, laptop ultrasottili, smartwatch, dispositivi IoT** (Internet of Things) for the smart home, voice assistants like Alexa and Google Home, and much more. Our screens are high definition or even 4K, a quality unthinkable in the era of cathode ray tube monitors with 800x600 resolution. Computer graphics have reached photorealistic levels, supporting virtual and augmented reality experiences.

Also the **software** today it is much more complex and feature-rich, but paradoxically often easier to use thanks to intuitive and standardized user interfaces. Modern operating systems (Windows 11, macOS, Linux in its user-friendly distributions, Android, iOS) offer superior stability and security, with frequent updates. Much of the software now is **oriented towards online services**: web applications, **cloud computing** and Internet-connected mobile apps. In the 1990s, most programs were installed locally and worked offline; today many tools reside on remote servers (the "cloud") and we can access them from any connected device. For example, personal storage has moved from local physical drives to cloud services such as Google Drive, Dropbox, OneDrive, etc., ensuring accessibility and synchronization everywhere. The counterpart is that we depend on the network: without an internet connection many of our daily applications lose functionality.

The **connectivity** in fact it is the pillar of today's technology. We went from analog modem to connections **broadband**, fiber optics and networks **4G/5G** cell phones. The result is that access to the

Internet has become instant and pervasive. Today beyond **67% of the world population** uses the Internet

en.wikipedia.org

; in absolute numbers it means more than **5 billion** of connected people

en.wikipedia.org

. In 2000 there were only ~400 million

elon.edu

. This exponential growth has made possible the era of social networks, video/music streaming, global e-commerce and many other innovations that were previously impractical. A person from the 90s would be amazed to discover that today we can watch a movie in high definition streaming on our phone while traveling by train, or have a free video call with relatives on the other side of the world: things that were science fiction then or simply impossible with the infrastructure of that period.

Another key aspect of today's technology is convergence and **miniaturization**. In the 1990s, separate devices were used: mobile phones for calls, pagers for short messages, Walkman or

Discman for music, film cameras for photos, video cameras for videos, dedicated consoles for video games. One today **smartphone** it combines all these functions: it is a telephone, a high-resolution digital camera, a multimedia player, a gaming platform, a GPS navigator, a personal diary and even a digital wallet. The power of its hardware and the intelligence of its software (often powered by AI for functions such as facial or voice recognition) make it a true digital Swiss army knife. As noted in a technology analysis, this has **"democratized"** access to computing capacity previously reserved for research centers or large institutions, putting "**immense computing power literally in our hands**" (enormous computing power literally in our hands) blog.adobe.com

.

In summary, current technology is characterized by: extremely powerful and interconnected devices; software capable of managing enormous amounts of data; widespread accessibility that includes billions of people; digital services that permeate every daily activity (from communication to work, from entertainment to health). This evolutionary leap has opened up extraordinary opportunities - think of advances in medicine thanks to information technology, or the possibility of learning online for free - but it has also created new dependencies and vulnerabilities, as we will see in the chapters dedicated to privacy and security.

Chapter 3: Technological evolution: from 1990 to today

After describing the technological scenarios of the 90s and today, we can highlight the **key aspects of evolution** that brought us this far. In just over a generation we have seen spectacular improvements in **performance, miniaturization, costs, diffusion and connectivity**.

One of the main drivers of this evolution was – as mentioned – the continuous increase in **computing power** according to Moore's exponential law blog.adobe.com
. In the 1990s the pace of development of microprocessors was impressive: clock frequencies doubled within a few years and the number of transistors grew even faster. For example, the 1993 Intel Pentium processor had ~3 million transistors and ran at 60 MHz; today an Apple M1 chip has 16 billion transistors and frequencies around 3 GHz, with multicore architectures and specialized coprocessors. Not only are the processors faster: the **memory capacity** has exploded (from RAM MB to GB, from disk MB to

SSD TB) and the **bandwidth** of connections has increased thousands of times (from 56k modem to 100 Mbps or 1 Gbps fiber connections, i.e. over 10,000 times faster). A curious comparison: a user remembers having bought a 40 MB hard disk for $240 in the early 1990s, while today with just a few dollars you can buy tens of GB of flash memory.

healthdatamanagement.com

, a sign of how the cost per unit of memory has collapsed.

In addition to pure power, the **miniaturization** and energy efficiency have allowed the advent of increasingly smaller and more powerful portable devices. In the 1990s, even imagining having current technology, it would not have been possible to build a smartphone: the components would have consumed too much energy and generated too much heat. Today, however, we have CPUs and chips designed specifically for mobile devices (such as ARM architectures) that provide high performance with low power consumption, making "pervasive" computing possible that accompanies us everywhere.

Another key aspect is the growth of **communication networks**. The adoption of global protocols (TCP/IP for the Internet), the expansion of infrastructures (undersea cables, satellites, cellular networks), and the evolution from 2G standards to 5G in mobile, have created a global connective tissue. If in 1990 only a tiny fraction of the world's population could access the Internet, today, as seen, we are above 60%. There **digital globalization** has become reality: information, ideas, goods and services circulate instantly online across national borders. In 1995 less than 1% of the world's population was online; in 2015 we were almost at 50%.
en.wikipedia.org
; in 2021 the threshold of 5 billion users was reached (about 2/3 of the human race)
en.wikipedia.org
. This spread also reduced the **digital divide** between countries, even if differences remain (in developed countries over 80-90% of the population uses the Internet, in less developed countries still only 20-30%
en.wikipedia.org
).

Along this evolutionary path some have occurred **technological breakthroughs** worthy of note. For example, the introduction of **World Wide Web** (first graphical browsers and websites in the 1990s) made the Internet usable by the general public. The advent of **search engines** (from Altavista to Google in the late 1990s) revolutionized the way we find information. The release of the first **iPhone** in 2007 it marked the beginning of the modern smartphone era, integrating telephone, internet and multimedia into a single touchscreen device. Progress in **lithium ion batteries** they have fueled the mobility of modern gadgets. On the software side, movement **open source** (also born in the 90s, think of Linux in 1991) has favored collaboration and open standards, accelerating innovation and access to code.

Finally, a transversal element that has characterized recent technological evolution is the growing importance of **data** and their "intelligent" processing. With the increase in power and connections, the amount of data generated and exchanged has grown enormously (we speak of **era** of **"Big Data"**). This has created both opportunities - for example the possibility of analyzing complex phenomena, of personalizing services, of training algorithms **machine learning** – and challenges in terms of management, privacy and security of the data themselves. From this one **data explosion** and today's computing capacity was born **Artificial intelligence** advanced, which we will talk about in the next chapters.

In summary, the technological evolution from 1990 to today can be seen as a process of **exponential acceleration** in many areas: more power, more miniaturization, more connection, more data. This has made technology more and more **ubiquitous** (anywhere and at any time) e **pervasive** in society, transforming not only the tools we use but also our behaviors, the economy and culture. With these foundations in place, we can now focus on the specific role of artificial intelligence, which has drawn inspiration from this evolution and has emerged as perhaps the most disruptive of current technologies.

Chapter 4: The advancement of Artificial Intelligence

L'**Artificial Intelligence (AI)** is a field of computer science that aims to create systems capable of carrying out tasks that would require human intelligence, such as learning from experience, reasoning, solving problems, understanding natural language, recognizing visual patterns, and so on. Although the term "Artificial Intelligence" was coined in the 1950s and there were cycles of enthusiasm and stasis ("AI winters") during the 20th century, it is above all in the last decades that AI has made extraordinary progress, thanks to the increase in computational power, the availability of large amounts of data and new algorithms (in particular **deep neural networks** o deep learning).

In the 1990s, AI was still largely confined to research laboratories and a few specific application areas. We worked on expert systems (rule-based programs to emulate decisions of specialists), on algorithms **machine learning** classics (such as few-layer neural networks, decision trees, fuzzy logic) and on restricted applications (for example OCR optical character recognition systems, or rudimentary statistical automatic translators). An important historical moment was 1997, when the IBM supercomputer **Deep Blue** defeated the world chess champion Garry **Kasparov** in an official match

ibm.com

. Deep Blue was actually a "brute force" combinatorial research system dedicated to chess, but that event had enormous media coverage: for the first time a machine beat a human being in a game considered a paradigm of strategic reasoning. Deep Blue's victory was seen as *"a turning point (inflection point) that heralded a future in which supercomputers and AI could simulate human thought"*

ibm.com

. In reality, AI in the late 1990s was still far from general human thinking; Deep Blue itself "reasoned" with brute force (analyzing millions of moves per second). However, that feat was testament to advances in specialized hardware and algorithms, and spurred further investment in AI research.

In the 2000s, AI continued to advance. An emblematic event was the **2011**, when an IBM system called **Watson** took part in the American television quiz show *Jeopardy!* challenging the two greatest human champions ever and managed to **WIN** the competition
ibm.com
. Watson was a system of **question-answer in natural language**: He could understand questions asked in ordinary English and find the correct answer by analyzing huge textual knowledge bases. This result marked a leap in **Natural Language Processing (NLP)**, showing that a machine could "understand" and answer complex questions more accurately and quickly than humans, at least in a domain like encyclopedic trivia. As noted by IBM, it was *"a great leap forward in a subbranch of AI called natural language processing"*, demonstrating the potential of machines capable of interacting by answering questions of all kinds
ibm.com
. After the victory, Watson technology was applied to fields such as medicine (to aid diagnoses based on medical literature) and business.

The truth **gear change** for AI, however, it arrived in the first half of the 2010s, with the renaissance of **deep neural networks**. In 2012, a deep neural network model (with many layers) named **AlexNet** won an image recognition competition (ImageNet) by a landslide, showing a drastic improvement over previous methods in classifying objects in photos. This achievement, along with similar successes in speech recognition, marked the beginning of a wave of deep learning adoption. The **GPU** (graphics processing units), originally designed for video games, turned out to be great for training neural networks due to their ability to perform mass parallel computations. In just a few years, AI-based computer vision and speech recognition systems reached and exceeded human performance in specific tasks in accuracy. A graphic published on *Our World in Data* shows that within **less than ten years** (2010-2020) we went from no machine with performance comparable to humans in image recognition or understanding language, to **AI capable of surpassing humans** in standard tests in these areas
ourworldindata.org
. In a short time, the machines learned to **view**

(identify faces, road signs, medical diagnoses on imaging) and a **hear/speak** (recognize the voice and respond).

Another memorable historical moment was the **2016**, when **AlphaGo**, a program created by Google DeepMind, defeated world champion Lee Sedol in the game of **Go**, an ancient oriental board game considered much more difficult than chess due to its complexity. AlphaGo combined deep learning techniques with advanced search algorithms and was trained in part by playing millions of games against itself. AlphaGo's 4-1 win over Lee Sedol was hailed as *"a significant milestone in the development of AI"*, given that Go was considered the last bastion of human intelligence in strategic games wired.com

. This success confirmed that machine learning methods had reached a level that could handle extremely complex tasks in creative ways (AlphaGo performed moves defined as "brilliant" and unexpected even for Go professionals).

Since then, advances in AI have continued apace. We saw it born **virtual assistants** such as Siri

(2011), Google Assistant (2016), Alexa (2014), capable of interacting with the user by voice; **self-driving cars** experimental vehicles capable of traveling on real roads; increasingly accurate automatic translators (such as Google Translate); and above all, recently, the systems of **Generative AI**. In 2022 the company OpenAI presented **ChatGPT**, an advanced chatbot based on a large language model (GPT-3.5, then GPT-4), capable of holding articulate conversations, answering questions and even creating original texts on request. In parallel, neural networks such as **DALL-E** the **Stable Diffusion** they showed the ability to generate new images starting from a textual description. These generative AIs have impressed the general public with their almost "creative" ability, opening up new possibilities but also ethical questions (originality of the works, risk of automatically generated disinformation, etc.).

In summary, AI has moved on from performing in **single and very limited tasks** (like playing chess) to permeate **many practical applications**. Although there is not yet a "general AI" comparable in versatility and self-awareness to the human mind,

AIs **"narrow"** today have achieved astonishing results: they see, listen, speak, translate, guide, play, diagnose, advise. In the next chapter we will see concretely how these AI capabilities have already entered the daily lives of most of us.

Chapter 5: AI in everyday life

Without often realizing it, we interact with artificial intelligence systems dozens of times a day. AI is the silent engine behind many commonly used services and devices. Let's see some examples of how AI pervades our daily lives:

- **Smartphones and voice assistants:** Almost all smartphones today integrate a virtual assistant (such as **Google Assistant** on Androids or **Siri** on iPhone). When we ask with the voice "What will the weather be like tomorrow?" or we dictate a message, voice recognition and sentence interpretation are performed by AI algorithms trained on huge linguistic datasets. If we take a photo, the camera software often uses AI to recognize the scene (portrait, landscape, night) and automatically optimize parameters such as exposure. Smartphones also use the **facial recognition** (Apple's Face ID for example) to unlock the device: behind this function there is a neural network that compares the face image in real time with a learned model of the user's face.

- **Web search and spam filters:** Every time we type a query into Google or Bing, a sophisticated algorithm **ranking** also based on AI, it determines the most relevant results, learning from the billions of searches carried out previously. Likewise, email uses intelligent spam filters that analyze email content and sender/recipient behavior to distinguish legitimate emails from spam or phishing: these filters are based on machine learning techniques trained on huge amounts of labeled email data.

- **Social media and streaming platforms:** When we scroll through the Facebook, Instagram, TikTok or Twitter feed (X), the order of the posts we see is not chronological but determined by algorithms **recommendation**. These AI algorithms consider our interests, past interactions, similar content liked by similar users, etc., to show us the most "engaging" posts. On YouTube or Netflix, AI suggests which video to watch or which

series to start based on our tastes: it analyzes our history and that of millions of other users to predict what we might like. This has a huge impact on how we consume information and entertainment - sometimes positive (we discover relevant content) other times problematic (personalized "bubbles" can be created or consumption habits reinforced, sometimes favoring extreme content to maintain attention
edri.org
).

- **E-commerce and personalized advertising:** If we visit Amazon or an online store, we are often shown advice like "You might also be interested in...". They are recommendation systems that use AI to match our behavior with general purchasing patterns. Even the **online advertising** it is targeted by AI: platforms such as Google Ads or Facebook Ads use algorithms to select the most relevant advert for each user in real time, based on their profile and click probability. This *micro-targeting* advertising is powerful

but has attracted criticism, especially when used in politics: the famous case of **Cambridge Analytica**, a company that used the personal data of millions of Facebook users and AI tools to create tailored political messages and potentially influence elections, demonstrating the dark side of advanced profiling
politico.eu

politico.eu

.

▢ **Maps and navigation:** Services like Google Maps or Waze use artificial intelligence both to calculate optimal routes and to predict traffic. By cross-referencing GPS data from millions of phones in real time, they are able to estimate road congestion and suggest alternative routes. Additionally, features like the *recognition* of places in photos (for example Google Lens which identifies monuments or restaurants from an image) or the instant translation of road signs framed by the camera are made possible by artificial

Jason Mallory

38

vision and multilingual translation models.

- **Banks and finance:** Many banks employ AI systems to detect fraudulent transactions: the algorithm learns to recognize atypical patterns (e.g. using the credit card in two different countries within a few minutes could suggest cloning) and can block suspicious transactions. In the context of **financial trading**, a large part of trades are performed by automatic algorithms (algorithmic trading) that make decisions in fractions of a second according to learned or predefined rules. Even in customer services, they are emerging **chatbot** banking or insurance companies that answer common questions via chat or phone, thanks to advances in NLP.

- **Health and Wellbeing:** AI is starting to support doctors and patients. Applications on smartphones can analyze health parameters (from heart rate to sleep) and provide advice. In diagnostics, computer vision algorithms analyze X-rays, MRIs and other medical images to detect early signs of disease (from fractures to tumors) with accuracy sometimes equal to that of a human radiologist. In some hospitals, AI helps optimize resource management, predict patient flows or suggest personalized treatment plans based on electronic medical records.

These examples show how AI *"Hides in plain sight"* in many ordinary aspects. And the trend is increasing: a study in the United States found that **99% of American adults have used at least one popular AI service in the past week**, even though only a third of them were aware of using artificial intelligence technologies
news.gallup.com

news.gallup.com
. This means that AI has now become basic infrastructure, a bit like electricity: we don't think about it, but it powers many tools we rely on.

Naturally, the widespread use of AI in everyday life brings with it tangible advantages: convenience (tailored services, automation of tedious tasks), efficiency (fast responses, optimization of routes and resources), expanded access (everyone can have an "assistant" 24/7), but also new issues. In particular, as we will see, there is the risk of depending too much on machines in important decisions, or of seeing one's behavior manipulated/subconsciously guided by algorithms about which little is known. Subsequent chapters will delve deeper into these issues by analyzing economic impacts, implications for work, privacy challenges, and ethical and human rights considerations related to ubiquitous AI.

5.1 International initiatives and regulations

At an international level, governments and supranational bodies have recognized the need for a coordinated approach to address the challenges posed by AI. In recent years they have emerged **global principles and guidelines** which establish shared values and guide national regulations:

- ⬜ **OECD (OECD)**: In 2019, OECD countries – joined by other G20 states – adopted the first *Principles on Artificial Intelligence*. These principles commit to developing AI that respects human rights and democratic values, promotes inclusive growth and well-being, is transparent and explainable, robust and safe, and subject to human accountability. whitecase.com

  whitecase.com
  . The OECD encourages one approach **"human-centric"** (human-centered) e **"risk-**

based", or calibrated on risks: systems with greater impact require more guarantees. These principles - the first ones also signed by economies such as the USA, the EU, Japan and even China and Russia - constitute a reference for many subsequent policies. For example, the definition of "AI system" in the future EU regulation is based on the OECD one

whitecase.com

.

- **UNESCO**: In 2021, all 193 UNESCO member states have approved the *Recommendation on the Ethics of Artificial Intelligence*. This is the first global regulatory instrument on AI, albeit non-binding. The recommendation establishes that the protection of human rights and dignity is at the heart of AI

  unesco.org

  unesco.org
  . Its principles include: respect for privacy, elimination of bias and discrimination, ensuring diversity and inclusion, guaranteeing

safety and environmental sustainability (the recommendation in fact recalls the need to reduce the environmental impact of AI systems). It also calls on states to take practical measures, such as ethical impact assessments before implementing AI in certain contexts, AI literacy programs for citizens, and even the creation of national AI registries or oversight bodies. Although it does not have the force of law, this document exerts moral pressure on governments and offers a comprehensive framework that several countries are using as the basis for their own strategies.

▪ **Council of Europe**: The Council of Europe (a pan-European human rights organisation, distinct from the EU) is developing a **Convention on AI, Human Rights and Democracy**. A convention, similar to the European Data or Cybersecurity Convention, would be legally binding on signatory states. The working group (CAHAI) indicated that the convention could set specific obligations to ensure that the use of AI is compatible with

the European Convention on Human Rights.
There is discussion, for example, of banning
AI applications that are contrary to
fundamental rights, of providing mandatory
impact assessments and effective remedies
for those who suffer unfair automated
decisions. If this convention is adopted
(possibly in 2024-2025), it will constitute the
first international treaty specifically on AI,
imposing common minimum standards in
areas such as facial recognition, profiling,
public sector decision-making systems, etc.

- **G7 and G20**: International leaders of major
  economies have integrated AI into their
  agendas. The *G20* of Osaka 2019 officially
  adopted the OECD principles on AI as a
  reference for member countries
  whitecase.com
  . In the *G7*, a "Global Partnership on AI"
  (GPAI) was launched to foster cooperation
  projects on responsible AI between countries
  and private stakeholders. The 2023 G7 (Japan
  Presidency) inaugurated the**Hiroshima AI
  Process**, a multilateral dialogue focused on

the risks of generative and advanced AI, which will lead to shared recommendations in 2024. Furthermore, the last G7 envisaged the creation of common standards for the safety assessment of frontier AI models.

- **Global AI Safety Summit**: In November 2023 the UK hosted the first global summit dedicated specifically to AI safety at Bletchley Park. Delegations from around 28 countries (USA, China, EU, India, etc.) participated together with experts and big tech. The *Declaration on AI Safety* emerging from the summit officially recognizes that advanced AI systems could pose significant risks, including extreme risks (the concept of risks to humanity is explicitly mentioned). The signatory countries undertake to collaborate on AI safety research and governance measures. Initiatives such as a have been announced **Evaluation network** joint - laboratories to test frontier models - and periodic meetings similar to the summit to update strategies
whitecase.com

<u>whitecase.com</u>

. While not producing immediate obligations, this summit marks an unprecedented global convergence on the need to monitor and manage the evolution of the most powerful AI.

- **Technical standards and private guidelines**: In parallel with government initiatives, entities such as **ISO/IEC** and **IEEE** are developing international technical standards (e.g. ISO IEC 42001 for AI management systems, IEEE 7000 standard for ethical considerations in the design of intelligent systems, etc.) with the aim of offering common methodologies for audit, documentation, risk assessment. Multi-stakeholder consortia like the **Partnership on AI** (which includes companies, academics and NGOs) have developed voluntary guidelines on topics such as fairness, explainability, AI governance, which often anticipate regulation. For example, the Partnership on AI has published recommendations on the use of AI in media and content moderation that are being considered by regulators.

Overall, a certain is emerging from these initiatives **international consensus on fundamental principles** for trustworthy AI: respect for human rights, non-discrimination, transparency, **appropriate human control** systems, responsibility and traceability, technical security and privacy protection
whitecase.com

whitecase.com
. At the same time, it is recognized that it is necessary to balance these guarantees with the promotion of innovation and investment in AI (no country wants to nip economic and social opportunities in the bud). Hence the orientation towards an approach **gradual and risk-based**: Many jurisdictions distinguish between AI systems **at high risk**, to be strictly regulated, and low-risk applications, for which general guiding principles suffice.

The challenge remains to avoid a fragmented landscape of divergent rules that make compliance

difficult for global companies
whitecase.com

whitecase.com
. To date, regulatory strategies differ: the EU has chosen a horizontal law (the future AI Act), the USA for now sector guidelines and investments in standards, China targeted regulations and state control (we will see details in the following sections). Bodies such as the OECD, the G7 and the Council of Europe try precisely to **harmonize** these approaches. For example, the definition of "AI" varies between jurisdictions
whitecase.com
, but we try to make it converge; the EU has aligned its (in the AI Act text) with the OECD and Canadian ones, while other countries (UK, Israel, Japan) avoid rigid definitions and prefer a flexible approach
whitecase.com

whitecase.com
.

In the absence of a single binding treaty at the UN

level, international principles are likely to serve as the basis and the various regional blocs will implement compatible regulations. The risk of a **fragmented regulatory environment** it's real whitecase.com

whitecase.com
, but initiatives such as the security summit and bilateral collaborations (e.g. EU-US dialogue in the Trade and Technology Council on AI) aim to avoid contradictions. For example, we discuss **common certification standards** of high-risk AI systems, so that an audit done in the EU is recognized in the US or vice versa.

In summary, at a global level there is a set of shared values for AI and a trend towards a **coordinated approach**: International ethical principles act as a compass, while each jurisdiction constructs its own detailed rules, ideally aligning them with that framework. The next few years will be crucial to see whether these regulations will converge towards a "common ground" (as happened for example with the privacy rules inspired by the GDPR in various countries) or whether fragmentation with distinct regulatory blocks will prevail. Meanwhile, in the following section, we look in particular at the European Union's regulatory proposal, which is the most advanced and ambitious one to date.

5.2 Legislation in the European Union: the AI Act and other initiatives

The European Union has placed itself at the forefront in the attempt to regulate Artificial Intelligence in an organic way. Building on the pioneering experience it had with the GDPR on privacy, the EU has adopted a regulatory approach aimed at creating **trust** in AI and a **harmonized single market** for products and services based on it. The core of this strategy is the proposal of **AI Regulation (AI Act)**, presented by the European Commission in April 2021 digital-strategy.ec.europa.eu
. The AI Act - currently in the final stage of negotiation between Parliament and the Council, with final adoption expected in 2024 - represents the first attempt in the world at horizontal and risk-based regulation of AI.

The salient features of the AI Act are:

   ▢ **Wide scope of application**: Will apply to **all AI**

systems placed on the EU market or used in the EU (even if developed elsewhere), in many private and public sectors. Defines an "AI system" broadly, including software developed with machine learning techniques, symbolic logic, or statistical approaches to generate outputs (predictions, recommendations, decisions) that influence real-world environments
whitecase.com

whitecase.com
. This definition, based on the OECD one, means that it includes not only neural networks and deep learning, but also rule-based systems, advanced optimization algorithms, etc., as long as they carry out tasks typically considered "AI".

- **Risk-based approach**: The AI Act classifies AI applications into four categories:

    1. **Prohibited systems**: a few specific applications deemed contrary to EU values. For example, **AI that uses subliminal or manipulative techniques**

to distort the behavior of individuals in harmful ways, massive **"social scoring" systems** (on the Chinese model) which evaluate the reliability of citizens with unfavorable effects
it.wikipedia.org

it.wikipedia.org
, and – with some exceptions – the use of **real-time facial recognition in public spaces for law enforcement purposes** (the EU Parliament has asked for it to be banned completely, except for searches for missing persons). These practices, considered to pose a high risk to rights and freedoms, will be prohibited.

2. **High risk systems**: they are the heart of regulation. The AI Act lists two annexes with types of applications considered "high risk" if used in certain contexts. For example: AI for recruitment or personnel management (due to the potential impact on working life), credit scoring systems, AI diagnostic medical devices, algorithms used in court to

assess recidivism, autonomous vehicle piloting systems, etc. The inclusion criteria concern the impact on security or fundamental rights. These systems will be permitted, but subject to **rigorous requirements** and to one **conformity assessment procedure** before placing on the market digital-strategy.ec.europa.eu

digital-strategy.ec.europa.eu

.

3. **Limited risk systems**: include most applications, such as chatbots, recommendation systems in streaming media, business diagnostics, etc. For them the AI Act provides only some **transparencies** (for example if we interact with a chatbot, the user must be informed that it is AI and not a human) and **voluntary codes of conduct**. So no stringent obligations, but encouragement to good practices.

4. **Minimum risk systems**: everything that does not fall into the other categories

(e.g. anti-spam filters, AI video games, low-impact applications). These remain essentially unregulated from the specific point of view of the AI Act (of course general laws, e.g. on product safety or consumption, continue to apply).

▢ **Requirements for high-risk systems**: Vendors (developers) and sometimes distributors/users of high-risk AI will have to comply with a number of obligations before and during use. Among the main ones:

1. Implementation one **risk management system** for AI, analyzing possible adverse impacts and adopting mitigating measures.
2. Guarantee **data quality** used to train, validate and test the system, to reduce bias and discriminatory results digital-strategy.ec.europa.eu
.
3. Keep one **detailed technical documentation** (the so-called "technical file" on the model of CE markings)

which allows the authorities to understand how the system is designed and why it complies.

4. Ensure an adequate degree of **explainability** and transparency: for example, providing information to end users on how to use the system correctly and its limitations.

5. Implement measures **human oversight**: this means designing AI so that human operators can monitor it and intervene if necessary, avoiding a scenario of uncontrolled autonomy whitecase.com

whitecase.com

.

6. Guarantee **robustness, safety and precision**: the system must be tested to resist attack attempts (e.g. adversarial inputs) and function reliably under expected conditions. Any malfunctions must have minimized impacts.

Before placing a high-risk AI on the market,

the supplier will have to carry out or have carried out an **conformity assessment** (in many cases self-declaration, in others - e.g. medical devices, AI toys - with a third party notified body involved). If it meets the requirements, it will affix the specific CE marking for AI. The system will then be registered in a **EU register of high-risk AI systems** managed by the Commission for Public Transparency.

- **Sanctions**: The AI Act provides a penalty regime similar to the GDPR. Violations of prohibitions or failures to comply with high-risk systems can result in fines of up to 30 million euros or 6% of the company's global annual turnover (whichever is greater) digital-strategy.ec.europa.eu . This gives considerable deterrent force. Each Member State will designate competent authorities (e.g. market surveillance authorities, digital guarantors) to supervise the application of the regulation.

- **Obligations for generative systems**: An element introduced in the most recent debate (2023) concerns i **generative AI models** GPT type. The European Parliament has proposed classifying them as "high risk" (given the potential for the spread of misinformation, plagiarism, etc.) and imposing specific requirements: for example, that generative models be trained on carefully controlled data to respect copyright and that their outputs include watermarks or other forms of identification.

whitecase.com

. In the final negotiations of the AI Act, the introduction of an ad hoc sui article is likely **Foundation Models**, which imposes transparency on data sources and obligations to mitigate general risks (bias, disinformation) before such models are made available.

In parallel with the AI Act, the EU Commission also presented an **new Directive on product liability** updated to include AI systems, and is developing a **Law on AI in military and security services** (sector not covered by the AI Act). Furthermore, a *High Level Expert Group on AI* who had published the

Ethical guidelines for trustworthy AI, outlining the principles that have largely flowed into the AI Act and policies such as the European AI Strategy.

The AI Act also aims to **strengthen the innovation ecosystem**: the EU will finance *"regulatory sandboxes"* where startups and entities will be able to experiment with innovative AI systems with temporary exemptions and under supervision, to test their compliance in a controlled environment (avoiding bureaucracy hindering innovation). Incentives and support are provided for SMEs to adapt to the new rules.

If the AI Act comes into force (after a transitional period of around 2 years), the EU will have a unified regulatory framework on AI. This – similarly to the GDPR – could become one **de facto standard** at a global level: tech companies that want to operate in the rich European market will have to comply, and perhaps they will adopt those measures elsewhere too. Already partners such as Japan and Canada have shown interest in aligning. It should be noted that the AI Act, being a regulation, will be directly applicable in all Member States without the need for transposition, ensuring uniformity.

However, there is no shortage of challenges: there is the risk that too burdensome rules will suffocate European startups, or that poorly calibrated provisions will quickly become obsolete in the face of technological evolution.
whitecase.com

whitecase.com
. For this reason, the EU is actively involving industry and academia in the final stages and has provided mechanisms for updating the annexes (for example to add new applications to the high risk list in the future). The declared intent is to replicate the "virtuous circle" seen with the GDPR: creating trust among citizens in AI (for example by ensuring that AI in sensitive areas is controlled) and therefore encouraging its large-scale adoption.

In parallel to the AI Act, it should be remembered that the **GDPR** already impacts various aspects of AI – for example by imposing transparency and the right to explanations in the case of significant automated decisions – and that sectoral regulations (e.g. Medical Device Regulation for medical AI, Consumer Products Directive, etc.) will continue to apply. The AI Act is designed to be complementary, filling specific gaps related to AI.

In conclusion, the EU with the AI Act is seeking a difficult balance: **protect values** (rights, security, equality) and together **stimulate innovation** in the digital ecosystem. If successful, it will establish a regulatory model for others to follow, contributing to convergent international governance. European regulation, risk-oriented and human-centred, embodies in legal form many of the ethical principles discussed globally.

whitecase.com

whitecase.com

. Much will then depend on the practical application: the authorities will have to have technical skills to evaluate complex systems, and companies will have to adopt a true "culture of compliance" integrating ethical and safety considerations right from the design (the so-called *"Ethics by design"*). The AI Act will therefore provide not only rules but also an impetus towards more development **responsible** of Artificial

Intelligence in Europe and, as a driving effect, perhaps in the world.

5.3 Policies and guidelines in the United States

In the United States, home to many of the big tech players in the AI revolution, the approach to regulation has so far been more decentralized and oriented towards guidelines rather than general laws. The USA does not (yet) have a comprehensive federal law on AI like the European AI Act, but over the last few years some **national strategies, executive directives and sectoral initiatives** to manage the opportunities and risks of AI.

A significant step was taken in **October 2022**, when the White House (Office of Science and Technology Policy) published the **Blueprint for an AI Bill of Rights**
bidenwhitehouse.archives.gov
. This document – not a law, but a set of principles and best practices – outlines **five rights/expectations** that citizens should have towards AI systems: (1) **Safe and effective systems** (AI should be tested for safety and effectiveness and monitored to mitigate harm); (2) **Protection against algorithmic bias** (systems should be designed and operated so as not to discriminate

based on race, gender, etc., ensuring fairness)
bidenwhitehouse.archives.gov

bidenwhitehouse.archives.gov
; (3) **Data privacy** (users should have control over their data, and AI systems should protect privacy by default); (4) **Transparency and explanation** (Individuals should know when they are interacting with an automated system and understand how and why it affects them)
bidenwhitehouse.archives.gov

bidenwhitehouse.archives.gov
; (5) **Human intervention options** (there should be human fallbacks: for example the possibility to turn to a person in case of a disputed algorithmic decision). The Blueprint serves as **ethical guide** for federal agencies and businesses: for example, the Biden administration has encouraged the various departments (transportation, health, justice, defense) to adopt these principles in their internal policies on the use of AI.

At the same time, at the beginning of 2023 the **NIST (National Institute of Standards and**

Technology) published the **AI Risk Management Framework (AI RMF 1.0),** a technical document that provides a voluntary standard approach to identify, assess and manage risks of AI systems. The NIST framework, developed with industry input, is intended for companies and organizations to implement trustworthy AI. It includes maps of possible risks (e.g. bias in datasets, adversarial vulnerabilities, impacts on civil rights) and suggests controls and processes to mitigate them, along the entire AI life cycle. While it is voluntary, the US government actively promotes it and many companies adopt it as best practice. For example, the AI RMF is designed similarly to NIST cybersecurity frameworks: it could be requested indirectly by government clients or as a basis in possible liability lawsuits.

On a real regulatory level, **the US landscape is fragmented**:

- At the federal level there is no general law on AI. It was preferred to issue for now **sectoral laws** or strengthen existing agencies. For example, for self-driving cars there are DOT (Department of Transportation) guidelines and some bills in Congress (not yet approved) for specific safety standards; for the healthcare sector, the FDA has issued guidelines on how to frame medical algorithms within the device regulator; the Equal Employment Opportunity Commission (EEOC) is addressing the issue of staff hiring and evaluation algorithms with respect to current anti-discrimination laws. The Federal Trade Commission (FTC), for its part, has made clear that it will use its sanctioning power against unfair practices related to AI (for example, if a company falsely claims that its AI product has no bias, constituting false advertising, the FTC can intervene). The FTC has also published guidance on *"AI transparent, fair and safe"* and warned businesses to avoid the so-called **"washed AI"** (AI washed of ethics only in words).

- At the level of **Federated States**, some have started to legislate in specific areas: for example, Illinois has a law that regulates the use of AI in video job interviews (AI Video Interview Act) imposing transparency and consent; Vermont and Alabama have state commissions to study the impact of AI; other states such as California are considering regulations on deepfakes (especially in an electoral context) and on the transparency of chatbots (since 2019 California has had the "B.O.T. Act" which obliges to declare when a bot impersonates a human online in commercial or political contexts). In 2023, New York City introduced rules requiring anti-bias audits for automated recruiting tools. whitecase.com

whitecase.com
. This situation generates a potentially heterogeneous mosaic of definitions and requirements for companies
whitecase.com

whitecase.com
, fueling calls for a clearer federal standard.

Aware of the risk of fragmentation and delay compared to Europe, in the last year federal legislators have accelerated: the US Senate has held hearings and meetings with CEOs of big tech and researchers (e.g. Mark Zuckerberg, Sam Altman of OpenAI, etc.) to discuss possible legislation. There has been talk of creating one **federal agency for AI** that regulates the most advanced models – an idea supported by some senators such as Schumer – but the debate is still in its early stages. The US is likely to remain on a "light-touch" approach for now, preferring to support innovation and intervene with targeted laws only where necessary.

In the meantime, the Executive has issued a **October 2023 an Executive Order on AI** (Executive Order "Safe, Secure, and Trustworthy Artificial Intelligence"). This act, signed by the President, does not create new laws but binds federal agencies and guides the private sector. Among the noteworthy measures: requires companies developing "frontier" AI models (the most powerful ones) to **notify the government of safety test results** and in certain cases of **share templates for national security assessments with the government**, especially if related to biosecurity, cybersecurity or potential catastrophic risks. Additionally, the Order allocates funds and directs to develop standards for watermarking AI-generated content (to combat deepfakes and misinformation), to integrate fairness considerations into hiring and lending (instructing the EEOC, CFPB, and FTC to issue rules or guidance in this regard), and requires federal agencies to use AI responsibly (for example, by expressly prohibiting the use of indiscriminate facial recognition without safeguards in their processes). In practice, the Biden Administration is using executive tools to advance protection while waiting for Congress to legislate.

On the regulatory front, therefore, the USA currently favors **non-binding frameworks** (principles, voluntary standards) e **application of existing general laws** to IA cases (anti-discrimination, consumer protection, competition). This partly reflects a different philosophy: to avoid stifling innovation with ex ante rules and correct abuses ex post. However, the speed with which generative AI (like ChatGPT) posed visible problems has pushed for more interventionism. For example, a strong signal is the establishment in August 2023 of a joint working group between the

White House and Big Tech (OpenAI, Google, Meta, Microsoft, Amazon) in which these companies took **voluntary commitments** to implement security measures in their models (such as watermarking the generated content and sharing risk information with the government)
whitecase.com

whitecase.com
.

In the absence of a unitary federal law, the USA is focusing heavily on **technological and ethical leadership of the industry itself**. For example, Microsoft and Google have published their own AI Principles and established internal committees on AI ethics. There is a certain reliance on the fact that the market (customers and investors) demands reliable AI and that companies therefore spontaneously implement compliance measures (also in view of the EU AI Act, given the global reach of big tech).

It must be said that the American context is also influenced by geopolitical competition: being too regulatory rigid could - it is feared - cause us to lose ground compared to China in AI innovation. On the other hand, demonstrating leadership in responsible AI can strengthen the global position of US companies, especially among democratic partners. The United States is therefore moving with caution: for example, it has so far preferred flexible guidelines and technical standards (such as the NIST RMF) that companies can adopt progressively, rather than imposing rigid compliance by law.

It is possible that within a few years, especially driven by events (a serious accident caused by AI or international pressure), Congress will also promulgate framework legislation on AI. It could be inspired by the model of **"Institute of AI"** or an independent supervisory body. But at the moment, the US approach can be summed up as **"guardrails without brakes"**: set boundaries and encourage virtuous behavior, without introducing many formal prohibitions or permissions.

Ultimately, in the USA the regulation of AI is taking place through a mix of **soft law (guiding principles)** and **creative application of existing hard law**, with an increasing role for executive orders and agencies in filling gaps. This more agile but also less predictable approach contrasts with the more codified European one. It will be interesting to see whether they will converge over time: for example, if the EU AI Act comes into force, many US software companies will still have to adapt to those requirements to operate in Europe, and this could actually raise internal standards in the US too (the so-called "Brussels effect"). Already now the definition of high-risk AI and the concepts of algorithmic bias present in the US Blueprint are attracting a lot of European debate. Looking ahead, therefore, despite following different paths, the United States and Europe seem to be moving towards similar objectives **Trustworthy and rights-respecting AI**, which facilitates future global alignment.

5.4 Regulation in China: state control and

guided development

China, recognized as one of the superpowers of Artificial Intelligence, has adopted an approach to regulating AI consistent with its political model: **strong state intervention, emphasis on social stability and censorship, and simultaneously vigorous support for domestic industry**. In recent years, the Chinese government has issued a series of targeted regulations governing specific aspects of AI and the use of algorithms, in particular to protect (or control) the public and prevent abuse.

A milestone was the publication, in 2017, of the **Development Plan for a New Generation of AI**: a strategic document with which China declared the objective of becoming a world leader in AI by 2030. Alongside massive investments in research and incubators (estimated tens of billions of dollars), the plan underlined the need for a **regulatory structure** to ensure "safe, reliable and controllable" development of AI, in line with Chinese socialist values. This foreshadowed subsequent regulatory moves.

China's major AI regulations include:

- **Recommendation algorithm rules** (entered

into force in March 2022): China was the first country to specifically regulate recommendation algorithms (those used by apps such as TikTok/Douyin, WeChat, e-commerce platforms). These rules, issued by the Cyberspace Administration of China (CAC), require algorithmic service providers to **register your algorithms with the authorities**

whitecase.com

whitecase.com
, providing technical details. Furthermore, they require that algorithms cannot be used to spread content that endangers national security or public order (broad concepts under which the political control of information falls). They must also promote "positive energy" and not encourage addictions (for example, they are asked to limit algorithms that encourage excessive use in minors). Chinese users have obtained, from these rules, some rights such as deactivating personalized recommendations or selecting and removing tags used for profiling. It

should be noted that the registration of algorithms shares the operating secrets of giants such as ByteDance and Tencent with the state, strengthening the party's supervisory power. In 2023, Chinese authorities began publishing **lists of registered algorithms**, with short descriptions, giving at least formal transparency.

- **Regulation on deepfakes and "deep synthesis"**: Entered into force in January 2023, imposes restrictions on the use of technologies to generate falsified audio, photo or video content. Service providers that allow the creation of synthetic faces or voices must obtain the consent of the people involved and, in many cases, insert a digital mark (watermark) indicating that it is generated content.
whitecase.com
. This is to stem the risks of misinformation, defamation or scams (for example deepfake videos of Chinese politicians would clearly be illegal). Deepfakes that could "undermine

national security or the national image" are prohibited. It is a regulation that reflects Beijing's concern about the hostile use of deepfakes in the political sphere, but also about protecting citizens from fraud (a real problem in China with deepfake calls).

▢ **Measures for Generative AI**: As ChatGPT gained global fame, China — where access to ChatGPT is officially blocked — was quick to regulate content generation services such as chatbots and image generators provided by Chinese companies. In April 2023 the CAC issued draft rules, then finalized in July 2023 as **"Measures for the management of generative artificial intelligence services"** lw.com

eastasiaforum.org
. These measures require that generative model providers (such as Baidu's Ernie Bot, Alibaba's Tongyi, etc.) **comply with censorship laws**: the contents generated must reflect correct socialist values, not subvert the state order, not spread

pornography, violence or fake news. They must also prevent output that may discriminate based on ethnicity, race, gender and protect privacy. It is expected **model registration** to the authority if the service is aimed at the public. Compared to the initial draft, the final version has been softened a bit so as not to slow down the industry: for example, the more stringent rules apply only to generative services *generally available to the public*, while the *generative tools for internal or limited use* they are exempt china-briefing.com

china-briefing.com
. This encourages private innovation while maintaining control over mass-market services. The sanctions for those who fail to do so include fines and suspension of service. In fact, these obligations force Chinese models to integrate robust censorship filters: Chinese chatbots refuse to answer "sensitive" questions (politics, Tiananmen, Xinjiang) and soften formulations in line with state propaganda.

- ▢ **Other related regulations**: China already had a strict cybersecurity law in 2018 and in 2021 *Personal Information Protection Act* (the Chinese counterpart of the GDPR). These general laws also apply to AI: for example, the privacy law limits automated profiling if it produces decisions with significant impact on individuals (similar to the GDPR). Furthermore, automotive regulations require that data collected by intelligent vehicles (road cameras, Lidar) be stored in China and subject to national security controls. This impacts manufacturers of autonomous cars and smart cities. The government also published **ethical guidelines**: for example, in 2021 a national committee set out ethical principles for AI (similar to Western documents) such as fairness, privacy, human control - a sign that even in China there is attention to these issues, although declined in the local context.

The Chinese approach to AI can therefore be summarized in **"support development, prevent chaos"**. The government invests heavily in AI (including for surveillance and military purposes, it must be said), but it wants to ensure that AI does not escape political control. Regulation is **very prescriptive and centralized**: Companies must register algorithms and models, undergo security and censorship audits, implement changes requested by the State. In essence, the *Cyberspace Administration of China* acts as a super-regulator of AI, supported by the competent ministries (e.g. the Ministry of Industry for standard aspects).

This high level of control has pros and cons: on the one hand, it allows us to more effectively limit phenomena such as fake news and extreme bias (even if the "cure" is often political censorship); on the other hand, it could slow down innovation, especially among smaller startups that struggle to comply with onerous requirements. Some observers note that regulations such as those on recommendation algorithms could reduce the international competitiveness of Chinese apps if they limit their ability to customize. However, so far the Chinese giants (Baidu, Alibaba, Tencent, ByteDance) have adapted and remain at the forefront of several AI fields.

Furthermore, China also intends **influence global standards**: actively participated in ISO/ITU committees proposing definitions and standards in line with its vision. For example, it has promoted the idea of standards for "credibility labeling" of online content, which reflects its censorship practice; also on the use of facial recognition it pushes standards of accuracy that legitimize massive internal use.

It should be noted that the ethical dimension in China is often connected to the concept of "*public order*" and "*social harmony*". For example, the regulations talk about avoiding algorithms that "jeopardize public morality" or that "harm the mental health of young people" – broad concepts within which the authority can intervene at its discretion. AI is seen as a tool to support stable social development and**state ideology**. This is evident in the intensive use of AI in video surveillance: China has deployed smart camera networks to recognize faces and behavior in cities (the "Skynet" project), justifying this as a means to reduce crime and increase citizen safety, although it raises concerns of privacy and social control.

In conclusion, China is building a regulatory framework for AI that reflects its authoritarian-digital model: **strong government oversight and related restrictions**, unite a **strategic support for the industry** to make it a global champion. This differs from the West, where the regulatory focus is on individual rights and fair competition: in China it is mainly on national security, censorship and internal order. For global companies, this creates a peculiar scenario: an AI product working in China must comply with very different rules than those in Europe or the US. For example, ChatGPT is not directly accessible in China, and equivalent Chinese versions must comply with censorship rules; conversely, a Baidu Ernie Bot brought to the West would have to be "de-censored" to be acceptable.

It is interesting that, despite opposing political visions, there is some formal convergence on basic technical and ethical principles: Chinese documents also speak of fairness, transparency, etc. – but the practical interpretation diverges. There **global AI governance** will have to take these different models into account. For now, China continues on its path: creating its own rules and trying to enforce them as standards in countries in its sphere of influence. It will be crucial to observe how the Chinese and Western regulatory regimes will interact in the future: whether incompatibilities will emerge (for example on the safety certifications of AI products) or whether there will be at least minimal mutual recognition on some issues (for example the marking of deepfakes, which China, the EU and the USA paradoxically agree is necessary). In any case, China offers a model **"authoritarian AI regulation"**, where AI is strongly shaped and contained by the State, as opposed to the Western "liberal" model. This dichotomy reflects the broader technological and value competition underway.

5.5 Ethical principles and sector guidelines

In addition to formal laws and regulations, a fundamental role in AI governance is played by **ethical guidelines and self-regulatory initiatives**. In recent years, research bodies, professional associations, companies and non-governmental organizations have developed a multitude of documents that define principles and recommendations for responsible AI. These ethical frameworks often pre-empt the law, filling the temporary regulatory gap and then influencing the drafting of binding regulations.

One of the first and most cited was the document of **EU Expert Group on Trustworthy AI** (2019), which set out 7 key requirements: human intervention and supervision; technical robustness and safety; data privacy and governance; transparency; diversity, non-discrimination and equity; social and environmental well-being; accountability. These principles have become a reference for many organizations, and as seen have been incorporated into the EU AI Act. In fact, a certain general alignment has been created on a global scale: a 2019 study identified at least 84 sets of ethical principles for AI published by various subjects, finding convergence on concepts such as transparency, non-maleficence, justice, autonomy and privacy.

whitecase.com

whitecase.com

.

Some noteworthy initiatives:

- **IEEE Ethically Aligned Design**: The IEEE, the largest association of engineers in the world, has published a substantial document *Ethically Aligned Design* which offers detailed guidelines for incorporating ethical considerations into the design of autonomous and AI systems. It also launched a series of standards (IEEE 7000) on issues such as bias models (7003), transparency (7001), machine learning governance (7010) etc. The IEEE approach is to give engineers practical tools to translate abstract principles into methodologies (e.g. how to implement an internal ethics committee, how to document choices for transparency) - thus complementing legal regulations with technical standards.

- ▢ **Asilomar AI Principles**: In 2017, at the Beneficial AI Conference held in Asilomar (California), a group of scientists and prominent figures (including Elon Musk, Sam Altman, Stuart Russell) signed 23 principles on the development of beneficial AI. Such principles include: AI's ultimate purpose is to serve humanity, defense of human dignity, caution in developing self-improving AI, importance of cooperation between nations for security, etc. Although unofficial, these principles have formed the basis for movements such as *Future of Life Institute* and stimulated the debate on AI Safety globally.

- ▢ **Partnership on AI and business principles**: The Partnership on AI (in which companies such as Google, Facebook, Microsoft, Apple, OpenAI and organizations such as Human Rights Watch, ACLU, etc. participate) has created working groups on various topics: fairness, security, work and AI, etc., producing best practices and white papers. Likewise, individual companies have published their own *AI Principles*: Google for example in 2018 announced seven principles (similar to those mentioned: socially beneficial purposes, security, privacy, avoidance of bias, verifiability, etc.) and a list of applications that it will not prosecute (including fully autonomous AI weapons and rights-infringing surveillance technologies). These internal principles led, for example, Google not to renew a controversial military contract (Project Maven) after internal protests. Other companies (Microsoft, IBM) have created internal ethics committees and toolkits (IBM released the *AI Fairness 360 Toolkit* open source to measure and mitigate bias). These moves also serve to **convey trust** to the public and regulators, showing voluntary commitment.

- **Public sector and government guidelines**: Several countries have issued guidelines for the use of AI by government agencies. For example, the **United Kingdom** there is a *AI*

Procurement Guide which provides officials with ethical criteria for purchasing AI systems (require transparency from suppliers, consider discriminatory impacts, etc.). The **deer** with the OMB (Office of Management and Budget) released one in 2020 *Policy Guidance* for the use of AI in the federal public sector inspired by the principles of transparency and fairness. These guides help the public sector set a good example in responsible use and avoid implementations that are not aligned with values (for example, they promote the use of criminal risk assessment algorithms only if subjected to rigorous bias testing).

- **AI Ethics in universities and training**: An often less formal but crucial aspect is spreading AI knowledge and ethics among developers. Many universities have introduced courses on "AI Ethics" into computer science curricula. Organizations like *ACM* and *AAAI* (computing and AI associations) have updated their codes of ethics to include the responsibility of engineers to prevent misuse of AI and to report any risks. The practice of is encouraged **"Ethical Impact Assessment"** to be conducted in parallel with AI projects, similar to how in the biomedical field every experiment passes through an ethics committee.

In specific areas, sectoral guidelines arise:

- **Healthcare**: The World Health Organization (WHO) published 6 principles for healthcare AI in 2021, including human control, transparency, accountability and promoting equity.
  pmc.ncbi.nlm.nih.gov

  pmc.ncbi.nlm.nih.gov
  . Bodies such as the American Medical Association are working on how to integrate AI into diagnosis and treatment without compromising the doctor-patient relationship.
- **Transport**: ICAO (civil aviation) discusses guidelines for AI in aircraft control and drones; the UNECE (UN commission) has

approved technical regulations for Level 3 autonomous vehicles including requirements on how to signal system limits to the driver.

- **Financial sector**: Singapore's MAS and other financial authorities have created the "FEAT" (Fairness, Ethics, Accountability and Transparency) framework for the use of AI in financial services, which has been adopted by banks as a voluntary standard.
- **Armed forces**: Even militarily there are emerging codes of conduct – the US DoD published in 2020 its 5 ethical principles for military AI (which include responsible, traceable, governable use – for example the obligation of deactivation interfaces on autonomous systems) and created an internal body (JAIC, now integrated into the Chief Digital and AI Office) to ensure the application of these principles in war projects.

These sectoral guidelines often prelude to regulations: for example, good practices in the financial sector will flow into regulations on "AI and fair lending". In other cases they remain as soft law which companies and institutions adopt to demonstrate social conformity and prevent scandals.

In general, the **AI ethics** is becoming an integral part of the product life cycle: we talk about *"Ethics by Design"* similarly to "Privacy by Design". For example, companies like IBM and Salesforce have created tools to help developers spot biases in data and models, and to log AI decisions (audit trails) for accountability. A set of methodologies is maturing: bias audit, algorithmic impact assessment (AIA), red-teaming (testing an AI to discover vulnerabilities and improper uses before release). Some governments, such as Canada, formally require a *Algorithmic Impact Assessment* before a public agency implements a major automated system.

However, the effectiveness of these voluntary and ethical initiatives depends on the genuine commitment of the actors and on social pressures. In the absence of binding rules, not all entities follow them. For example, although non-discrimination principles are universal, it emerged that some systems (e.g. for personnel selection) had gender biases: a sign that the guidelines are not enough without independent checks. This is one reason why we are moving from soft law to hard law on various issues (e.g. the EU in its AI Act requires mandatory audits for hiring systems whitecase.com

whitecase.com
, something anticipated by guidelines but now made binding).

In conclusion, the **ethical and sectoral guidelines** they laid the value foundations of AI regulation. They created a common language (term like *accountability*, *bias mitigation*, *human-in-the-loop* are now globally understood) and raised awareness among developers and policy makers. Often regulations (such as those of the EU, USA, UNESCO) draw directly from these soft law principles. It can be said that AI ethics has played a anticipatory role, outlining a sort of *moral constitution* on which to then build civil laws.

It remains fundamental that these principles do not remain abstract: the ongoing challenge is to translate them into **standardized practices,** certifications, professional training, and credible enforcement mechanisms. In a certain sense, the *legal rules* (previous chapters) and the *ethical standards* (this chapter) are converging: the ultimate objective is that the development of Artificial Intelligence intrinsically integrates the consideration of ethical aspects, just as the engineering sector has learned over time to integrate considerations of safety and technical reliability. When the culture of responsible AI is fully mature, the ideal would be for legal obligations to be a minimum common denominator already respected almost automatically by the majority of actors, thanks precisely to the solidity of the internal guidelines and standards adopted. We are in transition to this scenario, with both top-down (laws) and bottom-up (ethics, self-regulation) efforts having to come together.

Chapter 6: Artificial Intelligence and Economy

Artificial intelligence is having and will have a profound impact on**economy** at various levels: from the productivity of companies, to the economic growth of countries, up to the distribution of wealth. Experts talk about AI as one **"new industrial revolution"**, comparable to the introduction of electricity or the steam engine in terms of how much it can transform production processes. We try to outline the main economic advantages and critical issues related to AI.

On the side of **advantages and opportunities**, AI promises first of all to **increase productivity**. AI systems can automate repetitive or data-intensive tasks much faster and at lower cost than humans. They can function 24 hours a day, without breaks, processing information and making decisions in fractions of a second. This could free up the human workforce from many tasks, allowing them to focus on more value-added or creative activities. According to the International Monetary Fund, we are *"on the brink of a technological revolution that could boost global productivity and growth and raise incomes around the world"*

1y Mallory

. Estimates from consultancy firms indicate that widespread adoption of AI could add **trillions of dollars** to the global economy in the coming decades. For example, IDC Research predicts almost **20 trillion dollars** of AI's contribution to the world economy by 2030

electroiq.com

. In practice, AI can make almost every sector more efficient: from agriculture (optimizing the use of water and fertilizers through predictive analysis) to manufacturing (intelligent robots in Industry 4.0 factories), from transport (optimized logistics, autonomous vehicles) to services (automated processes in banks, personalized recommendations in e-commerce).

AI can also **encourage innovation** enabling things previously impossible. In the scientific field, for example, machine learning algorithms help discover new drugs by analyzing vast molecular combinations, or optimize the design of new materials. In energy, AI manages complex electricity networks by improving the integration of renewable sources. In general, companies that

successfully adopt AI could develop new products and business models, creating added value. Not surprisingly, **98% of business executives** worldwide considers AI essential for their business electroiq.com
, a sign of a strong expectation of economic returns.

However, on the side of **criticality**, the impact of AI on the economy may not be uniformly positive for everyone. One of the main concerns is the effect on**employment** and on **income distribution** (a topic that we will explore further in the following chapter dedicated to work). In short, while AI increases productivity, it also risks **substitute** many workers in tasks that can be automated, at least in the short to medium term. The IMF notes how *"AI could replace jobs and deepen inequality"* if not managed with adequate policies
imf.org
. An internal IMF study estimates that **nearly 40% of jobs globally** both to some extent *"exposed"* to automation via AI
imf.org
. It is striking that, unlike past technological waves

which mostly concerned manual and repetitive work, current AI can also automate cognitive tasks and therefore affect **qualified professions**: what *"What distinguishes AI is its ability to impact highly specialized jobs"* imf.org

. In fact, a greater effect is expected in advanced countries: up to **60% of jobs in advanced economies** could be touched by AI imf.org

, while in emerging countries the share is lower (around 40%, and in poor countries around 26%) imf.org

. This is because in advanced economies there are more "digitizable" jobs, both office and professional (analysts, clerks, even doctors for some diagnostic activities).

Numerous studies have tried to quantify how many jobs could **disappear** due to AI in the coming years. For example, a Goldman Sachs report (reported by the BBC) estimates that AI could replace up to **300 million jobs worldwide by 2030** electroiq.com

– about the**9% of global employment**. The World

Economic Forum predicts, in its "Future of Jobs Report", that by 2027 approximately 83 million jobs will be eliminated as a result of automation/AI, but at the same time ~69 million new ones should emerge, with a negative net balance of ~14 million

electroiq.com

electroiq.com
. McKinsey estimates that by 2030 up to **375 million workers** (14% of the global workforce) will have to change jobs or update their skills to adapt to automation

electroiq.com
. These figures should be taken with caution, but they outline a scenario of **forte disruption** in the labor market and therefore in the economy.

Another potential effect is the increase in **economic inequalities**. AI could give a huge advantage to **"Front-runner" countries and companies**, that is, those who have the capital, skills and infrastructure to develop and exploit it, while others may be left behind. For example, large technology multinationals (often US or

Chinese) are amassing enormous amounts of data and computing power, strengthening near-monopolistic positions in some sectors thanks to AI's economies of scale. This can stifle competition and channel wealth to a few players. Even at the worker level, AI could **polarize incomes**Highly skilled workers capable of using AI will increase their productivity (and wages), while those with easily automatable tasks will see demand and wages fall.

imf.org

. The IMF warns that *"in many scenarios AI will tend to aggravate overall inequalities"*, and that measures need to be taken to avoid it (social safety nets, training and retraining, redistributive policies) imf.org

.

Finally, in the macroeconomic context, AI also raises questions of **policy**: how to tax the value created by automation (for example, there are those who propose a "robot tax"), how to update economic indicators (does GDP adequately capture the contribution of AI?), how to prevent crises if financial algorithms behave in unexpected ways.

We also talk about the bargaining power of **data**: Nations that have more data to train AI (for example, those with large populations or less restrictive privacy laws) could benefit economically.

In conclusion, AI is powerful **engine of economic growth**, but not without side effects. On the one hand it can lead to a new wave of prosperity, better products, more efficient services and new industries. On the other hand, it risks concentrating the benefits too much among those who control the technology, creating imbalances in the world of work and in the distribution of income. The challenge for humanity will be to maximize gains in terms of overall wealth while maintaining the economy **inclusive**, ensuring that the fruits of automation are shared and that new jobs and opportunities are created to replace obsolete ones. As the director of the IMF, Kristalina Georgieva, effectively summarizes, a balance of policies must be found to *"safely exploit the enormous potential of AI for the benefit of humanity"*
imf.org

6. Social and Ethical Impact: challenges for society and man

The increasingly pervasive adoption of Artificial Intelligence in society poses not only technical and regulatory questions, but also profound challenges **social and ethical**. In this chapter we will analyze some of the major impacts of AI on the social fabric and values: from the protection of **privacy** of citizens in the era of big data, at the risk of **algorithmic discrimination** and perpetuation of bias in AI models; from the possible ones **digital inequalities** created by access (or lack of access) to advanced technologies, up to the implications on **relationship between man and machine**, or how AI affects our role in work and life, on our decision-making autonomy, on the very definition of humanity. These issues are the subject of public debate and growing attention from sociologists, ethicists, economists and the general public, because they touch on very concrete aspects of people's lives: fundamental rights, social justice, dignity and self-realization.

It is important to underline that AI, in itself, is not "good" or "bad" on an ethical level: it is a tool. But the way it is designed and used can generate beneficial or harmful outcomes. Society is faced with the task of **maximize the benefits of AI** – in terms of efficiency, new opportunities, improvement of services – e **minimize potential harm and injustice**. This requires not only laws (which we talked about in the previous chapter), but also cultural changes, empowerment of the actors who develop and use AI, and informed participation of citizens in choices on how to integrate it into daily life.

In the next paragraphs we will therefore examine four macro-areas of social impact: (1) the **privacy** and the management of personal data in the age of AI; (2) the phenomenon of **algorithmic biases and discrimination**, with examples of cases where AI treated some groups impartially or unfairly; (3) the new ones **digital inequalities** that AI could accentuate or alleviate – from the access and skills gap to the impact on the labor market and the distribution of wealth; (4) the change in

relationship between man and machine, including the topic of the role of human work alongside automation, the trust/risk in delegating decisions to machines and the transformations in the way we interact and perceive increasingly "intelligent" artificial entities.

6.1 Privacy and surveillance: AI between opportunities and risks for personal data

In the age of AI, the **privacy** has become a central and complex theme. On the one hand, artificial intelligence can be used to protect privacy - for example, advanced algorithms allow us to detect and prevent violations, manage consents in a granular way, anonymize data intelligently. On the other hand, many AI techniques feed on enormous quantities of **personal data** and their effectiveness often depends on analyzing information about people in depth, raising concerns about surveillance and misuse of this data.

A clear example of privacy-AI tension is the **facial recognition**. Computer vision systems trained on billions of images can identify faces with high precision, which has useful applications (unlocking your phone with your face, finding missing people) but also potential abuse (constant tracking of citizens in public space, ethnic profiling). We have seen how in China facial recognition is integrated into the state surveillance system: intelligent cameras recognize individuals and behaviors, fueling sophisticated social control. Even in Western democracies, police forces have experimented with the use of this technology: in the United Kingdom and in some US states it has been tested on images from security cameras to identify suspects in real time. This has generated strong reactions: civil rights groups denounce that such practices undermine privacy and can lead to **mass surveillance** indiscriminate

whitecase.com

whitecase.com

. Furthermore, facial recognition errors and biases are documented: studies (such as that of NIST 2019) have highlighted that many algorithms have *false positive* much more frequent for ethnic minorities, especially people of color, than for Caucasian faces

en.wikipedia.org

en.wikipedia.org

. This has already led to mistaken arrests of African Americans in the US due to mistaken identifications. Thus, numerous American cities (San Francisco, Boston) have banned the use of facial recognition by local authorities. The EU, as seen, is about to broadly ban real-time facial recognition in public spaces

it.wikipedia.org

it.wikipedia.org

, except for very narrow exceptions, precisely to protect the right to privacy and freedom of anonymous movement.

Another front is the **online profiling**. Digital platforms use AI to analyze our activity (clicks, likes, purchases) and draw detailed information on preferences, habits, political inclinations or even health conditions. This fuels advertising micro-targeting: for example, social networks can show extremely personalized adverts, or tailored content that captures our attention (sometimes accentuating phenomena such as *filter bubble* and radicalization). From a privacy point of view, although the data used often does not include name and surname, the **behavioral profile** which results is like a unique imprint of the person. The GDPR and other laws give users the right to be informed of this profiling and to object to it. But in practice it is very difficult to escape: most sites collect data via cookies or trackers; AI makes such data extremely "revealing". Let's think about the**inference of sensitive data**: An AI model can infer a person's sexual orientation with good accuracy by analyzing their likes on Facebook whitecase.com

whitecase.com
, or establish his mental health status from written posts. These practices raise ethical questions: it is one thing if the person has consciously consented to have this information deduced, it is another if the company does it behind the scenes for commercial purposes.

AI also enables multi-source correlations that are difficult to do manually: by combining different databases (credit card purchases, geolocations from apps, web history) you get an almost omniscient view of someone's life. Privacy guarantors fear the **re-identification**: Machine learning techniques can often re-identify people in seemingly anonymous datasets, finding unique patterns. For example, a study showed that with little data on "anonymized" credit card transactions an algorithm could trace the identity of a large part of individuals by crossing them with other datasets (because spending habits and times become a personal "signature").

Then there is the aspect of **automated decisions** that impact privacy and rights: for example, AI systems used by public bodies to evaluate whether to grant a visa, or by banks to approve a loan, could consider data collected in non-transparent ways (perhaps information on social media or purchases). The GDPR protects the right not to be subject to fully automated decisions that produce legal or similar effects, without the possibility of human intervention or challenge.
it.wikipedia.org

it.wikipedia.org
. This means citizens should be able to ask for

explanations and dispute, for example, whether an AI-determined credit score has disqualified them from a mortgage. However, asserting this right is not easy: often people don't even know that there is an algorithm behind the decision (hence the transparency requirements that regulations such as the AI Act and Blueprint USA strengthen).

AI also poses dilemmas **collective privacy and public environments**. For example, the use of drones with smart cameras to monitor crowds (as pioneered during the pandemic to verify distancing) was technically useful, but raised questions: Are we normalizing constant surveillance? Will we feel free knowing that we are being monitored by electronic eyes everywhere? Similarly, "social scoring" systems (citizen evaluation based on aggregate data) in the West are rejected because they are considered incompatible with privacy and individual autonomy, while in China they are presented as a tool for building trust and virtuous behavior. It is clear that AI amplifies the difference in vision between societies more oriented towards privacy and others more oriented towards control: the fear of many is that, if not adequately regulated, the technology (which is neutral) actually favors models of **Orwellian surveillance**.

An example on a local scale: a **London**, the public transport system uses AI to analyze passenger flows (Oyster card data, Wi-Fi tracking in stations) and optimize services. This improves efficiency, but has raised questions about what individual mobility data is stored and whether it can be used for different purposes (police, marketing). AI can do that too *erode privacy "de facto"*: perhaps legally the data is anonymous, but the aggregation and fine analysis makes them tools for surveillance of collective behavior.

Among positive opportunities, there is the **Privacy-Enhancing Technologies (PET)** based on AI: for example, algorithms *differential privacy* add calibrated noise to data to protect identities while ensuring statistical accuracy; Neural networks can be trained in a federated manner – data remains on users' devices and only updated parameters are shared and aggregated

whitecase.com

whitecase.com

(Google uses this to train predictive keyboard models without sending user messages to the server.) Furthermore, AI can help users manage their privacy: for example, personal assistants that understand the privacy policies of sites and automatically set optimal preferences for the user, or intelligent filters that warn you if you are accidentally sharing sensitive data on a social network.

Ultimately, the impact of AI on privacy is twofold: **enormously enhances the ability to analyze and monitor**, but it also provides new tools to protect and give control. The balance will depend on how we balance these aspects. So far, lawmakers have responded with regulations like the GDPR, California's CCPA, and the like, strengthening data subjects' rights and imposing limits (consent, specific purposes, data minimization). But AI evolves quickly: for example, there is discussion about whether to allow law enforcement agencies to use AI on large communication datasets to identify terrorist threats (a bit like the film *Minority Report*). *How far to go?* Society will have to decide how much value to place on privacy versus other benefits. Already during COVID-19 we have seen differences: Asian countries with extensive electronic tracking (often with AI for cluster analysis) have contained the virus better but with costs for privacy; Europe has chosen tracking apps that are more respectful of anonymity (decentralized Bluetooth) while accepting less effectiveness. Similar choices will present themselves.

In summary, the **challenge privacy** in the age of AI consists of **maintain control over your data and identity** in a context of ubiquitous and invisible computing. This requires constantly updating safeguards (technical, legal) and ensuring that AI is used to emancipate the individual and not to reduce him to an object of analysis or commercial target. A complex balance, constantly evolving as AI becomes increasingly integrated into the devices and environments around us (intelligent IoT, smart cities). Preserving spaces of anonymity and personal privacy could become an increasingly difficult and valuable challenge.

6.2 Algorithmic discrimination and bias: is AI unbiased?

One of the most studied ethical issues related to AI is the risk of **algorithmic discrimination**, that AI systems treat certain groups of people unfairly, often reflecting or even amplifying existing prejudices in society. In fact, AI is not intrinsically fair or impartial: it learns from the data we provide it and from past human decisions. If these data or decisions contain bias (prejudice, imbalance), the algorithm risks reproducing them on a large scale and with an aura of objectivity. Furthermore, even with "clean" data, certain models can identify spurious correlations that indirectly penalize protected categories.

Concrete examples of **algorithmic bias** which have emerged in recent years have become emblematic case studies:

- **Personnel selection systems**: In 2018, it was revealed that Amazon had developed a recruiting algorithm to skim CVs, but had to discontinue it because it was found to discriminate against women whitecase.com

whitecase.com

. The model had been trained on the company's historical hiring data (male-dominated tech sector) and had learned, implicitly, that male candidates were preferable. As a result, it penalized CVs that contained words like "women's chess club captain" or degrees from women's colleges, and gave lower scores to women. This shows how AI can *inherit the prejudices of the past*: if a sector had a gender bias in the past, the algorithm perpetuates it unless corrective interventions are made. New York City responded to similar cases by introducing a groundbreaking rule in 2023 that mandates **annual independent audits on bias** for automated personnel selection tools used by companies

whitecase.com

whitecase.com

.

☐ **Criminal justice algorithms**: In the US, some

courts and prisons use risk assessment systems (such as COMPAS) to estimate a defendant's likelihood of reoffending, aiding judges in decisions about probation or parole. A 2016 ProPublica investigation showed that COMPAS tended to incorrectly classify blacks as "high risk" much more than whites. en.wikipedia.org

en.wikipedia.org
. Notably, among those who did not commit subsequent crimes, blacks were labeled high risk at double the rate of whites (44% vs. 23%). Conversely, among those who later relapsed into crime, whites were often wrongly judged to be low risk. This suggests a racial bias: the model (fueled by historical arrest and conviction data, itself known to be influenced by racial disparities in the American justice system) penalized people of color. The COMPAS case has sparked a huge discussion about **algorithmic fairness** and has led some states (e.g. California) to review or limit the use of such tools. The problem is complex because the concepts of statistical

fairness are multiple and sometimes incompatible with each other (COMPAS, for example, was calibrated to have the same global accuracy on whites and blacks, but this produced disparities in false positives). This has led to the search for more suitable fairness metrics and the recommendation to use risk assessments only as an aid, not in a deterministic way.

- **Bias in image recognition and digital services**: An episode that became famous was when, in 2015, the Google Photos algorithm incorrectly labeled two black people as "gorillas" in the images en.wikipedia.org

  en.wikipedia.org
  . This sparked outrage: it was a model error (due to inadequate training set and possible data bias) with offensive racist connotations. Google took action by apologizing and improving the dataset, but this and other incidents (such as automatic soap not detecting a black person's hand, or a

camera's AI describing Asians with closed eyes as "blinking") have highlighted how AI products launched without adequate diversity testing can cause offense and discrimination.

⬚ **Credit systems and dynamic prices**: Algorithms that determine interest rates on loans or insurance could, even without using ethnicity or gender as an explicit variable (which would be illicit), end up systematically penalizing some groups through proxy variables (e.g. postal code of residence, spending patterns). For example, a model could offer worse conditions to those who live in certain socio-economically disadvantaged areas, which perhaps correlate with ethnic minorities, thus falling into indirect discrimination. Similarly, in online marketing and e-commerce there is discussion as to whether personalized pricing AI could make certain categories pay higher prices (perhaps identified as less sensitive to price or, on the contrary, as "wealthy"), creating unequal treatment of consumers based on factors such as area or device used (there have been cases of sites offering different prices to those who browsed on a Mac compared to a PC, assuming a different purchasing power).

The theme of **bias** it is broad and does not only concern protected categories such as race and gender, but also possible disparities towards the elderly, people with disabilities, linguistic minorities, etc. For example, voice assistants initially struggled to understand strong accents or the speech of people with speech impediments, effectively excluding them from equal access to such services. Only by working on more inclusive data and universal design can we improve (today the accuracy of voice recognition for female voices remains slightly lower than that for male voices, due to data historically unbalanced towards male timbres).

Addressing algorithmic discrimination requires actions at multiple levels:

- **Technician**: development of algorithms *fairness* and debiasing. There are now numerous methods to measure unequal treatment (equal opportunity, equalized odds, fairness through thresholds, etc.) and ways to mitigate them, for example by rebalancing the training dataset, applying fairness constraints during model optimization, or correcting the output by calibrating the scores for different groups. Research in fairness-ML is very active. For example, an open source tool from IBM (*AI Fairness 360*) provides dozens of metrics and algorithms to detect and reduce bias. However, there is no single solution: often improving fairness with respect to one criterion can worsen other parameters (e.g. slight decrease in general accuracy), so a compromise and value choice is needed (e.g., do we prefer a slightly less accurate model but which reduces racial disparity? In many ethical cases, the answer tends to be yes).

▪ **link**: As mentioned, regulations are emerging. Anti-discrimination law already prohibits discrimination based on certain characteristics – now it is a matter of adapting it to the algorithmic context. In the USA the *Equal Credit Opportunity Act* was invoked by the CFPB to investigate potential biases in credit scoring. In the EU, the AI Act will require assessments and documentation for high-risk systems to prevent discriminatory impacts digital-strategy.ec.europa.eu

digital-strategy.ec.europa.eu
. Furthermore, transparency regulations help: if an algorithm has to explain the factors that led to a decision, it is easier to identify discriminatory elements and contest them.

- **Diversity in teams**: An often cited factor is that teams developing AI should be diverse. If only one demographic plans, they risk not seeing problems affecting other groups. Having engineers, designers, and ethicists from different backgrounds can surface possible biases early. For example, the Google Photos gaffe probably would have been caught sooner if the testing had also been conducted by people of color in key roles.
- **Community involvement**: The idea of is taking hold *co-design* with the impacted

communities. For example, if a city wants to implement an AI system to allocate social services, involving representatives of disadvantaged communities in the criteria-setting and testing process helps avoid disparities. External auditing by independent third parties (academics, NGOs) is also crucial for credibility: companies like Facebook have commissioned civil rights audits to assess the impact of their algorithms on minorities.

It should not be assumed that algorithmic biases are always evident: they often are **thin**. For example, a language model might more frequently associate leadership or STEM career terms with male names (reflecting gender stereotypes in training texts) – this subtle correlation can then creep into outputs (translations, completions) that perpetuate the stereotype. Real case: machine translation systems in languages without grammatical gender (e.g. Turkish) tended to translate sentences like "o bir doktor" (means "he/she is a doctor") into "He is a doctor" and "o bir hemşire" ("he/she is a nurse") into "She is a nurse", reflecting the man-doctor, woman-nurse stereotype. Google Translate and others have had to step in to provide inclusive translations ("He/She is a doctor") to avoid gender bias. This shows how biases can manifest themselves in small, everyday things, influencing cultural perceptions.

Ultimately, the goal is **IA mare** (*fair AI*), which treats similar individuals equally and does not penalize protected categories. Even knowing that a completely neutral AI can be utopian (also because the data reflects a non-neutral society), efforts can and must be made to get as close as possible. As a report from the Berkeley AI Institute wrote, *"bias in data is not an excuse: the responsibility of those who develop AI is to recognize and correct them, because the large-scale use of AI risks cementing prejudices if we do not intervene"*. The challenge is made even more critical by the fact that AI decisions can be opaque: so a hidden bias could go unnoticed for a long time while affecting many lives. Hence the importance of frequent audits and the principle of *accountability* (i.e. someone - the company, the institution - must answer for the decisions of the system and its possible prejudices

whitecase.com

whitecase.com
). Only by combining technical progress, intelligent regulations and social awareness will we be able to avoid the danger that AI becomes an amplifier of discrimination rather than a tool for reducing it.

6.3 Digital inequalities and impact on work: AI and the social issue

The advent of large-scale Artificial Intelligence is reshaping the contours of the economy and work, raising hopes but also fears regarding the **inequalities**. On the one hand, AI has the potential to increase productivity, create new professional opportunities and improve access to essential services (personalized education, low-cost healthcare through automated diagnoses) by reducing some disparities. On the other hand, there is concern that AI could accentuate the gap between those who have the skills and capital to exploit it and those who are excluded, as well as lead to polarization in the labor market (some highly skilled and creative professions thrive, many repetitive and medium-level tasks disappear).

A first dimension of inequality concerns the**digital access and skills**. Countries and regions with advanced technological infrastructures and strong investments in AI could further distance themselves from less developed areas. A significant gap already exists today: according to recent data, around 13% of the world's population does not have access to the internet. AI — particularly applications such as language models, automation systems — tends to be concentrated where there are large datasets and computational resources (mainly North America, Europe, China). This risks marginalizing less digitalized countries: for example, if precision agriculture with AI increases yields in rich nations, poor countries that cannot implement it fall even further behind in agricultural productivity and food security. This **global inequality** it is the subject of initiatives such as AI4D (AI for Development) which aims to transfer knowledge and models adapted to local needs. But it is not trivial: current language models also support dozens of languages, yet many African or indigenous languages do not have sufficient corpuses and may be overlooked. There is a risk of "digital colonization" where local cultures and needs are filtered through models trained on data from dominant cultures.

In the world of work, AI sparks the debate on **automation** and possible technological unemployment. Numerous studies have estimated that between 10% and 30% of existing work tasks could be automated within 10-20 years thanks to AI and robotics. That doesn't necessarily mean net unemployment on that scale – technology has historically created new jobs while eliminating others – but it does herald a **difficult transition**. Some categories are particularly exposed: drivers (with the advent of autonomous vehicles), assembly line and warehouse operators (robots like those of Amazon already reduce the need for human warehouse workers), data entry and processing workers (AI software can analyze and summarize documents much faster), first level customer service workers (replaceable by advanced chatbots). A recent case: machine translation and text generation services like DeepL and GPT are reducing the demand for human translators for standard texts and copywriters for basic content; on the other hand, the demand for new professions such as "prompt engineers" (those who know how to best train generative models) or human reviewers who check and refine the automatic output is growing.

This transformation can generate **polarization**: jobs that are highly qualified, creative, or that require emotional intelligence and human interaction (e.g. strategy development, scientific research, personal care, arts) could become even more valuable and enriched by AI as a tool; conversely, many routine office jobs and some routine manual jobs may contract. The risk is an "hourglass" society: many highly qualified workers and a significant number in low-skilled jobs in personal services (which AI is unlikely to completely replace, e.g. carers, cleaners, etc.), with a contraction of the white-collar middle class.

The question **distributive** is crucial: AI could increase global productivity and therefore overall wealth, but how will this surplus be distributed? If the benefits are concentrated on the owners of capital (those who own the technologies, data centers and patents) and on an elite of highly specialized workers, economic inequalities could grow. Already today we can see a concentration of power in a few leading AI companies (Google, Microsoft, Amazon, Meta, Tencent, Alibaba...), and some estimates indicate that AI could push up the profits and salaries of top engineers, while reducing the market value of automatable tasks (with stagnation or reduction of salaries in those sectors). This scenario prompts reflection **new socio-economic models**: for example, the idea of a **universal basic income** it is often debated as a possible response to a future in which traditional human labor is not enough to employ everyone. Or models of *"flexicurity"* where the State or companies invest massively in the retraining of workers (reskilling/upskilling) to enable them for roles that are complementary to AI rather than replaceable by it.

There are also more optimistic visions: some analyzes (e.g. one by PwC 2018) suggest that AI will create more jobs than it will destroy, in particular by generating demand for professionalism in AI itself (developers, data scientists, ethics and governance experts), but also by increasing productivity so much that resources will be freed up to expand sectors such as education, healthcare, art and entertainment - all sectors with a high intensity of skilled human labour. However, this requires **active policies**: AI can relieve doctors and teachers of administrative tasks, allowing them to follow more patients or students, but investments are needed to hire more doctors and teachers, not cuts using AI as an excuse to save money. Therefore, governments have the task of directing the fruits of AI efficiency towards one **inclusive growth**

whitecase.com

whitecase.com

.

Another dimension of inequality concerns the **type** : While AI itself is neutral, the tech sector has historically had a significant gender gap (women are underrepresented in STEM and AI careers). There is a risk that the opportunities created by AI will be seized predominantly by men, perpetuating the salary and leadership gap. On the other hand, conscious policies can reverse the trend: for example, promoting female participation in AI training, encouraging female tech startups, and using AI to support social needs that often involve more women (e.g. AI for family assistance, efficient teleworking, etc.).

The **education and training** become key factors in order not to generate "digital exclusions".

Education systems need to be updated to prepare young people for an AI economy: this includes technical skills (from coding to data literacy) but also soft skills that AI is unlikely to replicate (creativity, critical thinking, empathy, teamwork). Paradoxically, as AI takes on mechanical tasks, typically human skills become even more important. A worker of tomorrow will perhaps have to know **collaborate with AI**: for example, a journalist will have to know how to use AI tools for research and drafting, but then put human quality into the finishing; a doctor will use diagnostic AI but will maintain the relationship with the patient and the final clinical judgment. This involves training workers to see AI as a **amplifier** of their capabilities, not just a competitor. The risk is that those who fail to make this leap will fall behind professionally.

Finally, a social aspect often highlighted is that of **meaning and dignity of work**. If AI reduces the need for human labor, how can we ensure people have a sense of role and belonging? Work is not just income: it is identity, status, routine. A society in which many were "technologically unemployed" with a guaranteed income could still present problems of cohesion and personal fulfillment. So some suggest reducing the overall working hours (for example the 4-day week) by distributing the remaining work among more people, accompanying with volunteering activities, continuous training, arts and sports to fill the free spaces. The transition must be thought of not only in economic terms but also of **psychological well-being**.

In conclusion, AI can both exacerbate and alleviate inequalities: it is a "multiplier" of trends and political choices. Without interventions, it could accentuate concentrations of wealth and opportunities in the hands of a few; with far-sighted policies, it could free humanity from burdensome work and improve everyone's standard of living. The outcome will depend on how governments, businesses and civil society manage this revolution. In a way, AI tests our ability to **adapt the social contract**: a new balance is needed between innovation, equity and social protection. The debate is open and today we are already seeing differentiated proposals: there are those who call for a "tax on robots" to finance the retraining of replaced workers, those who push for the open source of the fruits of AI (so that the benefits are not patented and monopolised), those who propose a "universal dividend" when highly automated companies achieve super-profits. It will likely take continuous experimentation and adjustment.

In any case, it is clear that AI requires us to rethink how to guarantee **social justice in the digital age** whitecase.com

whitecase.com
. It is not just a technological task but above all a political and ethical one: innovation must go hand in hand with social cohesion to prevent the society of the future from being technologically advanced but socially fractured.

6.4 Human and machine: cooperation,

dependence and identity

As Artificial Intelligence integrates into our lives, the line between what is "human" and what is "machine" becomes increasingly blurred. This raises questions about the **relationship between man and AI**: How will we interact and cooperate with intelligent machines? Will we become dependent on them to the point of atrophying certain of our abilities? And, more profoundly, will the advent of artificial entities equipped with advanced cognitive abilities lead us to redefine what it means to be human, what is our identity and our role in the world?

An immediate aspect is the **man-machine cooperation**. In many fields, from industry to healthcare, the AI paradigm is emerging *augmented intelligence*, that is, an intelligence that increases human capabilities instead of replacing them. For example, in a hospital, a radiologist supported by an AI algorithm diagnoses tumors with greater accuracy
pmc.ncbi.nlm.nih.gov

pmc.ncbi.nlm.nih.gov

and can focus on the most complex assessments; in the factory, specialized operators supervise teams of collaborative robots (cobots) that carry out repetitive tasks, as seen

weforum.org

. This cooperative scenario appears to offer the best of both worlds: the computational speed and precision of machines and human creativity, empathy and contextual judgment. However, it requires establishing **mutual trust** and clear protocols: the human must understand when to trust the AI and when to intervene, the AI must be designed to be transparent and understandable to the human. An airline pilot today interacts with AI-based autopilots: most of the flight is handled by automation, but the pilot must monitor and take charge if the AI fails. This has improved safety, but there have been cases of overconfidence or confusion about what the automation was doing that contributed to accidents (e.g. the Boeing 737 Max case and the MCAS system). This highlights the need to invest a lot in **usability and human-AI interfaces**: AI does not have to be an inscrutable black box for the human operator.

The **dependence** from AI is another concern. If we delegate more and more cognitive functions to machines (memorizing telephone numbers, orienting ourselves with GPS, remembering appointments, translating languages, deciding logistical routes, suggesting news and friends), do we risk losing skills and autonomy? For example, already today many of us would struggle to navigate a city without Google Maps again. In the future, with more sophisticated AI personal assistants (who perhaps organize our agenda, respond to our messages, choose for us what to watch or read based on our tastes), we could fall into a sort of *intellectual comfort* which reduces our capacity for conscious choice and active learning. Another area is the**education**: If students can have ChatGPT complete their written assignments, how can they ensure effective learning? There is discussion of using AI as a tutor to explain and improve, not to provide answers directly, precisely to avoid the atrophy of reasoning skills. Just as with the advent of calculators there was a debate about which mental calculation skills to preserve in teaching, with AI it is necessary to define which human skills should still be exercised. Some propose refocusing education on creativity, critical thinking and social-emotional skills, leaving "mechanical tasks" to AI.

Addiction can also take the form of **decrease in control**: If our lives become too orchestrated by algorithms, there is a risk of feeling less in control of our decisions. For example, if an algorithm constantly advises us where to invest our savings, what diet to follow, who to go out with, we could delegate profound personal choices to a system which, although based on our data, deprives us of exploring alternatives and free will. On this point there is an ethical reflection: the**autonomy** it is a key value - in medicine, for example, the patient always has the last word in therapeutic choices. Similarly, we should retain decision-making sovereignty in every context where AI offers us recommendations.

A particular aspect of the man-machine relationship is the question of**empathy and attachment** towards AI agents. Already now, many people give names to their voice assistants or home robots and treat them as quasi-friends. Studies have shown that lonely elderly users can draw emotional comfort from social robots (such as the robot puppy Paro). This opens up positive opportunities – AI like *companion* to combat loneliness, help in therapy (there are chatbots for psychological support, e.g. Woebot) - but also dilemmas: is it right to leverage an attachment towards entities that don't actually feel feelings? For example, if a voice assistant simulates empathy ("I understand that you are sad today, I'm very sorry"), the user could develop a one-sided emotional bond. As long as this has beneficial outcomes (feeling listened to) it could be fine, but there is the fear of **illusions**: Mistaking an AI's simulated "sympathy" for true understanding can further isolate you from genuine human interaction. Furthermore, if people begin to prefer interacting with docile and always available AI rather than with other people (who can be disagreeable, unpredictable), social skills could also atrophy. In short, a **balance between human and AI interaction** will be important for social health.

The last and perhaps most philosophical theme is that of**human identity** and the intrinsic value of humans in a world with advanced AI. If in the future (even a distant one) we were to live with an AI with intelligence comparable to or superior to ours (think of the strong AI or superintelligence scenarios discussed in chapter 4), how will this affect our collective self-esteem? Already with models like GPT-4, which in certain tests exceed the human average (it has passed professional exams, solves general knowledge problems better than many), there are those who feel a sense of *"algorithmic inferiority"*. However, there are also those who react by valuing even more the unique qualities of man: authentic creativity, conscience, spirituality, ability to improvise and give meaning to things. Perhaps the presence of intelligent machines will push us to clarify what really differentiates us: for example, the **free will** (if it exists) and the ability to feel authentic emotions and have subjective experiences (the famous qualia) are elements that – for now – we attribute only to living beings.

Scenarios also open up **man-machine integration**: as discussed with transhumanism, the possibility of cybernetic enhancements arises. Already pacemakers, cochlear implants and neuroprostheses are medical realities; in the future, brain-computer interfaces could seamlessly connect our brains to external AI systems. If this happened, the distinction between "human decision" and "AI suggestion" would become almost irrelevant: we would be one with AI support. This leads to a rethinking of personal identity: if part of my memory or analytical capacity resides on a chip, am I still fully "me"? Many transhumanists would say yes, simply broadening our definition of self; critics would say that we risk losing authenticity or becoming too dependent on technology even internally.

Finally, there is the appearance **cultural and existential**: jobs once reserved for human ingenuity – composing music, writing poetry, painting – can now be carried out by AI (albeit with variable quality). If AI produced better art and science than us, what would be the role of the human artist and scientist? Some find in this prospect a sense of dismay, others of liberation (we could dedicate ourselves to something else, or collaborate with AI to create even greater things). In any case, it forces us to reaffirm that the **value**

of the human being it does not reside only in productivity or computational ability, but also in irreducible elements such as sensitivity, moral conscience, the ability to appreciate beauty and experience the world. Paradoxically, AI could make us rediscover the importance of these qualities, shifting the emphasis of society from "doing" to "being" - if we are able to understand it in this way.

From a social point of view, avoiding a man-machine fracture means **orient the development of AI towards humans**: as often reiterated, AI should be a tool that *serve* humanity, not an end in itself. This concept of *"augmented humanity"* (human augmentation) suggests a future in which collaboration is close but the direction and goals are always defined by man, on the basis of his own values and aspirations. Educational, cultural and religious institutions have a role here: to accompany people in making sense of coexistence with AI, in maintaining the centrality of the human.

In summary, the human-AI relationship is a **delicate balance between autonomy and support**. There will be areas in which we will want to give up control (for example when driving, if autonomous cars prove to be much safer, perhaps we will prefer to leave it to them), and others in which we will always claim human choice (high-level ethical, judicial, creative decisions). Even within the person, there is a new balance between trusting one's own abilities vs trusting AI: for example in medical diagnostics, young doctors must be careful not to rely too much on AI and lose the ability to diagnose with their own head. The concept of *"de-skill"* (loss of skills) is already known in other automation contexts (pilots on autopilot, architects with CAD): with AI this phenomenon could extend. It will be the task of society and individuals to keep the "muscle" of ingenuity and creativity trained, despite having very powerful intellectual prostheses.

In conclusion, far from being relegated to science fiction, the theme of the man-machine relationship is very concrete and everyday: it involves how we will work, how we will decide, how we will relate and even how we will think about ourselves. It is one of the areas where the**practical ethics** will need to be more vigilant in the coming years to ensure that as we embrace AI we do not lose what makes us human.

Chapter 7: Artificial Intelligence and Work

The impact of AI on **Work** it deserves a dedicated analysis, being one of the most immediate and tangible aspects for millions of people. Automation via AI represents a continuation (and acceleration) of the technological changes that have always transformed the world of work. However, the scale and speed of this current transformation pose unprecedented challenges.

Potential benefits for the job

In optimistic scenarios, AI could **improve the quality of human work**. By automating the most repetitive, dangerous or exhausting tasks, AI can free workers from alienating tasks. For example, in warehouses, intelligent robots can take care of moving heavy loads; in manufacturing plants collaborative robots ("cobots") can carry out precision assemblies, reducing the physical efforts of workers; in offices, RPA (Robotic Process Automation) software can carry out routine administrative procedures (data entry, document verification) leaving supervisory and decision-making tasks to employees. This could lead to more jobs **safe**, less exhausting, with more space for creativity and human relationships.

Furthermore, AI can act as **capacity amplifier** humans, acting as "co-pilot" in many jobs. A doctor equipped with diagnostic AI tools can identify diseases more precisely and quickly (AI becomes a second opinion that analyzes thousands of images in a few seconds). A translator can use an automatic translation system for the first draft and then refine it. A teacher can use AI platforms to personalize student learning, adapting pace and materials to individual needs. In these cases AI **increases productivity** of the worker, allowing him to obtain better results in less time. Studies have shown, for example, that the use of AI language models can speed up the training of less experienced workers, helping them achieve higher levels of productivity more quickly
imf.org
. If implemented well, then, AI could lead not so much to a replacement, but to one **complementarity** man-machine, where human qualities (creativity, empathy, ethical judgement) combine with the calculation and analysis capacity

of machines.

It is also possible for AI to create **new jobs** and entire new professional sectors. History teaches that every great technological innovation initially eliminates some roles but generates new ones that didn't even exist before. In the field of AI we are already seeing the emergence of professions such as the data scientist, the machine learning engineer, the "prompt engineer" (someone who is expert in interacting with generative AI systems), the AI ethicist (expert in ethical implications). As AI spreads, figures will be needed to develop it, maintain it, explain it, regulate it. The World Economic Forum points out that alongside the jobs that will disappear, there will be tens of millions of new jobs **created** from emerging technologies electroiq.com

(for example software developers, AI specialists, robotics technicians, but also roles in "automation-proof" services such as personal care, education, artistic creativity which could grow). Another area in which AI could generate employment is that of **redevelopment**: trainers and instructors will be needed to update the skills of those who are displaced by automation and must learn new jobs.

Critical issues and risks for the world of work

However, there is no shortage of concerns, some
already mentioned in the previous chapter. The
most direct is the **technological unemployment**:
Many people could lose their jobs as they are
replaced by more efficient automated systems.
The sectors most at risk are those with **repetitive
and predictable activities**. For example, in road
transport there is discussion of the arrival
(although not imminent on a large scale) of self-
driving trucks that could one day replace drivers on
long journeys; in large-scale retail trade, automatic
checkouts and robotic warehouses reduce the
need for cashiers and warehouse workers; in
financial services, AI can process insurance or
credit paperwork that previously required
numerous workers. Even in the white-collar
context, **advanced chatbots** and automated
response systems could reduce the ranks of call
centers and customer service centers; smart
accounting software could decrease the need for
junior accountants; and so on.

As seen, some estimates speak of tens or hundreds

of millions of jobs potentially eliminated within a decade

electroiq.com

. Even if new ones were created in parallel, the **transition period** it could be traumatic. Not all dismissed workers will easily be able to retrain for more qualified roles; those who are close to retirement age or have low digital skills risk being left behind. This would lead to an increase in **structural unemployment** in some sectors and regions, with important social consequences (increased inequalities, discontent, tensions). Industrial history provides examples: deindustrialization without adequate retraining has left many areas in an employment crisis for decades. AI could amplify this effect if policies are not far-sighted.

Another critical issue is the **change in the nature of work** and possible worsening of conditions if AI is used improperly. For example, there is a fear of a future in which personnel management algorithms constantly monitor the productivity of each employee and optimize every second of their day, reducing autonomy and increasing stress. Already today in some warehouses and delivery companies, workers are guided by software that assigns tasks in real time and measures retail performance, at pace dictated by machines. This can lead to an alienating work environment, where humans are treated like a cog. Furthermore, the **gig economy** (platform work) uses algorithms to distribute tasks (e.g. Uber rides, Glovo deliveries) and this sometimes makes work precarious, with workers bound to the opaque rules of the algorithm. So AI in work also raises questions of **workers' rights**: transparency of management algorithms, limits to digital control, protection of the dignity and privacy of the monitored worker.

Then there is the question of **polarization of skills**. AI could increase the demand for highly specialized workers (engineers, developers, analysts, managers capable of integrating AI into the business) – who will likely see growing wages – while reducing the demand for workers with medium and low skills, who risk underemployment or less remunerative jobs. This trend was already underway with traditional IT automation, but AI could accentuate it because it is capable of performing even medium-level cognitive tasks. The result would be a world of work divided into "those with high skills win, those without them lose", worsening inequalities. A study on effects in the USA suggests that **80% of the US workforce** could see at least 10% of their tasks automated through advanced AI models

electroiq.com

, but this impact will not be the same for everyone: young people may adapt better, while older workers will struggle to reskill

imf.org

.

Adaptation strategies

Faced with these challenges, it becomes crucial to implement strategies so that AI is an ally of the worker and not an enemy. International organizations such as the IMF and OECD recommend **massive investments in training and retraining**: Governments and businesses should prepare programs to teach new digital and soft skills to at-risk workers, before they lose their jobs. THE'**education** it must be rethought to provide new generations with skills complementary to AI -

critical thinking, creativity, empathy, which machines do not yet have.

They will also serve **social protection measures** innovative: for example, if technological layoffs increase, it may be necessary to strengthen unemployment benefits, or imagine distributed reductions in working hours (making everyone work a little less, rather than leaving someone without a job, hypotheses such as the short working week). Some economists discuss universal basic income as a safety net in case automation dramatically reduces the availability of traditional jobs.

Another approach is to involve i **unions** and workers in the technological transition: agreements that provide that the adoption of AI in the company is accompanied by internal training and outplacement for those who are automated, rather than immediate dismissals. In some countries there is also discussion about giving workers representation in algorithmic choices: for example, **transparency on algorithms** of personnel management, right to contest decisions made by AI (such as negative evaluations or automatic dismissals decided by the algorithm).

Ultimately, AI does not inevitably condemn humans to a jobless future – rather, **it will change the jobs**. It is up to us as a society to drive this change in a way that is sustainable and humane. Historical experience suggests that, if well governed, technologies create more prosperity and even new jobs. But the transition period can be painful if unprepared. The key will be **proactivity**: predict the sectors at risk, train people in time, and redesign the labor economy so that it remains centered on human well-being. AI could thus become a liberating tool (reducing human fatigue) rather than a factor of alienation or exclusion.

Chapter 8: Artificial Intelligence and Privacy

The rise of AI raises important questions of **privacy** and protection of personal data. Many of today's AI technologies are based on the analysis of enormous amounts of data, often collected from individuals' online and offline activities. This poses the dilemma of balancing the benefits deriving from the use of such data (which allow AI to provide personalized services, accurate predictions, etc.) with the right of individuals to privacy and control over their own information.

One of the main critical issues is the **massive collection of personal data**. Every one of our digital interactions - searches on Google, posts on social media, purchases with a credit card, geolocations from the smartphone, images from security cameras in the city - can become input for AI algorithms. Technology companies have developed the ability to **profile** users in an extremely detailed way: AI sifts through "big data" to infer even sensitive information from our online behaviors, such as political interests, health status, intimate preferences, often without these having been explicitly provided. As the UN special rapporteur on privacy highlighted, profiling can be done through AI *"infer sensitive information about people that they have neither provided nor confirmed"*

edri.org

. For example, by analyzing likes on social media, an algorithm can predict a person's political orientation or sexual orientation with good accuracy; by cross-referencing location data and purchases, it is possible to understand daily habits, social relationships, any health problems (doctor visits, drugs purchased).

This **digital surveillance** for commercial or other purposes threatens the concept of privacy. Individuals often have very little control over what data is collected and how it is used. The privacy policies of the services are long and complicated, and in practice the average user agrees (perhaps without reading them) to give up a lot of data in exchange for the "free" use of online services. But behind the scenes, that data powers AI models for targeted advertising, for recommendations, or – in worse scenarios – can end up in the wrong hands via security breaches.

An emblematic case was the scandal **Cambridge**

Analytica of 2018, in which millions of Facebook profiles were collected without consent and used (with the help of AI algorithms) to target personalized political messages during election campaigns

politico.eu

. This event opened my eyes to the ease with which personal data can be exploited for **manipulate** public opinion, putting both individual privacy and democratic processes at risk. Following this and other cases, there is a growing demand for **regulation** more stringent on the use of data and AI (as we will also see in the next chapter on human rights).

In addition to the collection, there is the theme of **data storage and security**. If more and more personal information is entrusted to algorithms, it must be adequately protected from unauthorized access. A flaw in the databases that train an AI (think health data used for a medical AI) could expose confidential details of millions of people. And even when leaks do not occur, the problem of**secondary use** of data: data collected for a certain purpose (e.g. measuring steps on a smartphone for one's health) could be used for other purposes (an insurance company that wants to estimate a customer's health risk). Without regulations, AI enables these cross-analysis in ways that are difficult to track.

A delicate frontier is that of **facial recognition** and intelligent video surveillance. AI can analyze video streams in real time to identify faces and track people in public places. Systems have been tested in some cities around the world **mass surveillance** with facial recognition, justified as tools for security and crime prevention. However, civil rights organizations denounce that these technologies *"pave the way for mass surveillance"* politico.eu
and have called for moratoriums on their use, highlighting the risk of one **digital police state** where every movement of the citizen is tracked. In London, for example, police began using real-time facial recognition cameras in some areas in 2020, sparking legal challenges and public protests politico.eu
. Even when such systems are implemented with good intentions, the danger of abuse (to monitor

dissidents, minorities, etc.) is real, as examples in authoritarian countries where high-tech surveillance is used to control the population show.

In the commercial context, another problem is the **invisible tracking**. For example, many websites and apps use algorithms to "guess" information about the user and dynamically adapt content: this can lead to price discrimination (different prices depending on the profile), or to showing targeted content that limits the user's vision (e.g. personalized search results that exclude certain content). In short, AI can *"shaping the information world in a way that is opaque to the user"*, influencing what we see without us realizing it edri.org
. This has implications for both privacy (we don't know what data about us they are using to show us certain things) and decision-making autonomy.

Regulation and solutions

To address these risks, several regulatory and technological initiatives are underway. In Europe, for example, the **General Data Protection Regulation (GDPR)** which came into force in 2018 imposes strong constraints on the use of personal data: it requires explicit consent, the right to be forgotten, the obligation to inform about how the data is used, and establishes that an individual has the right to **not be subjected to automated decisions** (by AI) that have significant effects on him, without the possibility of human intervention. However, the GDPR is only a first step and does not specifically address AI, although it applies to data used by AI. At European level, the**AI Act**, a proposed regulation on artificial intelligence that includes bans on uses of AI considered to pose a high risk to rights (e.g. "Black Mirror"-style social scoring, or mass biometric surveillance), and transparency and evaluation obligations for other uses.

Other jurisdictions follow: countries such as Canada and China have enacted laws on personal data and algorithm governance, and in the US several states have privacy laws (e.g. California Consumer Privacy Act). Furthermore, there are ethical guidelines (e.g **Ethical Guidelines on AI** released by the European Commission and those of UNESCO) which recommend respect for privacy as a fundamental principle in the development of AI.

From a technological point of view, approaches are being developed **Privacy-by-design** for AI: for example techniques *federated learning* (federated learning) that allow you to train algorithms without centralizing the raw data (the data remains on local devices and only the aggregate parameters are shared), or the use of homomorphic encryption to process encrypted data without decrypting it. These solutions could mitigate the conflict between data use and privacy.

However, it also remains fundamental **user education**: make it clear what data they share, demand transparency from companies. For example, clarify that if a service is free, the product is likely user data; encourage the use of privacy settings and tools such as anti-trackers, VPNs, etc. when appropriate.

In conclusion, AI accentuates the dilemma between innovation and privacy. The ability to process mountains of data to extract knowledge involves a *cost* in terms of loss of individual control over their data. As a UN report stated, if left unregulated, AI can "call into question respect for privacy".

edri.org

. It is therefore vital to define clear limits: which uses of AI on personal data are acceptable and which are not; ensure that the user maintains the **digital sovereignty** on sensitive information; and ensure that AI is used transparently and responsibly by institutions and businesses. Only in this way will it be possible to benefit from AI without giving up the fundamental rights to privacy and informational self-determination.

Chapter 9: Artificial Intelligence and Human Rights

In addition to privacy, AI raises various ethical and legal issues **human rights**. International bodies, such as the United Nations, have begun to analyze the impact of AI on fundamental rights and to define principles for AI that respects human values. Let's look at some key areas of intersection between AI and rights.

Freedom of expression and information

As mentioned in the previous chapter, AI algorithms today significantly influence the information we have access to – for example through social media feeds or search engine results. This has consequences on the **freedom of expression and opinion**. On the one hand, the Internet and AI have democratized speech: anyone can express their opinion and find a platform, and AI can help surface niche content for interested audiences. On the other hand, however, AI can create **invisible filters** and echo chambers: as UN rapporteur David Kaye observes, AI *"shapes the world of information in a way that is opaque to the user"* and the personalization of content tends to

reinforce pre-existing biases, *"encouraging the promotion of sensational content or misinformation to keep the user engaged"*
edri.org
. This can limit information pluralism and condition the free formation of individual opinion, thus subtly threatening freedom of thought and expression.

Another aspect is the **online content moderation**. Given the amount of content generated by users, platforms such as Facebook, YouTube, Twitter increasingly rely on AI algorithms to filter illicit or harmful content (hate speech, terrorism, nudity, etc.). This is understandable, but automatic systems often make mistakes: they can remove legitimate speech by mistaking it for prohibited (false positives), or vice versa let disguised hate speech pass through (false negatives). Kaye notes that entrusting censorship to AI risks **undermine freedom of expression**, because the machine does not understand the context, the irony, the cultural nuances
edri.org
. For example, an algorithm could censor artistic or

denunciatory content that contains violent images "to raise awareness", treating them as apologies for violence. There is therefore a risk that "overzealous" automated moderation becomes a form of **preventive censorship**, compromising the right to inform and be informed. Some activists are calling for it to stay **human involvement** in moderation and that users can challenge decisions made by AI.

Non-discrimination and equality

A key principle of human rights is the right not to be discriminated against based on personal characteristics (race, gender, ethnicity, opinions, etc.). The use of AI in various fields (job hiring, service provision, judicial decisions, credit granting, police surveillance) can threaten this principle if the algorithms are not fair. Unfortunately, **many AIs have shown bias** discriminatory, reflecting biases present in the data on which they are trained or in the choices of their designers. For example, recidivism risk assessment software used in courtrooms in the US has been accused of disproportionately penalizing black defendants (all other factors being equal)

<u>edri.org</u>

. Facial recognition systems have proven less accurate at recognizing faces of women or ethnic minorities, leading to increased false positive identifications of innocent suspects among these populations. AI-based recruiting tools trained on historical data may unconsciously replicate stereotypes (for example, more easily discarding women's CVs for IT positions if past data hires were mostly men).

This happens because AI **it is not neutral**: Learns from real-world data, which is often far from fair. If the training data contains biases (conscious or otherwise), the algorithm internalizes them and amplifies them at scale. Furthermore, some machine learning techniques are like "black boxes", difficult to interpret even for the creators: this makes it difficult to identify and correct possibly discriminatory decisions. Delegating important choices to opaque processes conflicts with people's right to an **fair and transparent treatment**. The UN special rapporteur says that automated decisions can have discriminatory effects because *"by relying exclusively on specific*

criteria and not guaranteeing transparency, they can produce distorted outcomes"
edri.org

.

To address this, we discuss the need for **explainable algorithms** (*Explainable AI*) and independent audits of algorithms used in sensitive areas, to verify that they do not create disparities. Furthermore, some argue that in sectors such as justice or predictive policing the use of AI should be severely limited if not accompanied by robust guarantees, because algorithmic error can result in violation of rights (such as the unjust arrest of a person misidentified by software).

Right to life and personal integrity

An extreme but fundamental chapter is the application of AI in **war and security field**, which affects the right to life, security and safety. The advancement of AI has led to the development of **autonomous weapons** capable of selecting and hitting targets without human intervention (the so-called "Lethal Autonomous Weapon Systems", LAWS). Many experts and human rights activists call for the prohibition or strict regulation of such weapons, since delegating the decision to kill a human being to a machine poses serious ethical and legal problems. There is a risk that imperfect algorithms could cause civilian casualties, or that responsibility for any war crimes becomes elusive ("is it the algorithm's fault?"). Unethical use of AI in warfare could lead to violations of international humanitarian law.

Even in the civil sector, AI can threaten safety if it malfunctions: think of a self-driving car that causes an accident due to a software error - who is to blame? Who compensates the victims? This requires us to rethink **Legal frameworks on liability**.

Participation rights and transparency

The massive impact of AI on society raises the question of **democratic control** about these technologies. Human rights include the right of citizens to participate in public decisions and to have accountable institutions. If algorithms govern important aspects (from security to the distribution of resources), citizens have the right to know how they work and to demand that they are aligned with the values of the community. In some cases, governments' opaque use of AI could undermine public trust and the social contract.

For this reason, there is a growing movement for **AI Governance**: establish principles of transparency, accountability and **final human control** (the so-called "human-in-the-loop" or rather "human-in-command" for crucial decisions). Organizations such as UNESCO have produced documents such as **Recommendation on AI Ethics** (2021) in which they state that AI must respect human rights and that mechanisms for supervision and impact assessment are needed. The Council of Europe is developing a Convention on AI, human rights, democracy and the rule of law. All of these initiatives recognize that AI is not just a technical issue, but of **values and rights**.

In summary, AI can impact almost the entire spectrum of human rights: from privacy to freedom of expression, from equality to access to justice, from the right to life to political participation. It is not a subject of law (it is a technology), but its **consequences** require us to adapt our protection systems. AI developed and used without consideration for rights can amplify injustices and create new tools of oppression. On the contrary, an AI oriented by respect for rights can be an ally in promoting dignity and well-being (for example, facilitating access to information, helping people with disabilities through intelligent assistive technologies, etc.). It is up to humanity, through laws, institutions and ethical choices, **channel AI** towards the strengthening and not the erosion of universal human rights.

Chapter 10: AI in the future of humanity – prospects and challenges

After having explored the various aspects of technological evolution and artificial intelligence, we turn our gaze to the future: what could be the **role of AI in the humanity of tomorrow**? It is a vast topic that touches on different visions – from the utopia of a world powered by AI, to the dystopia of a society dominated by machines. Reality will likely fall in between, influenced by the choices we collectively make in the coming years.

Positive outlook: Many scientists and futurists see enormous potential in AI to solve global problems. For example, AI could accelerate scientific discoveries by helping to find cures for currently incurable diseases (by analyzing complex biomedical data, proposing molecules for new drugs). In the context of climate change, AI can optimize energy use, predict natural disasters and model interventions to mitigate global warming. AI could also help **defeat poverty** improving efficiency in agriculture (smart crops), education (personalised teaching on a large scale even in remote areas) and resource management. In an ideal future, dangerous or exhausting jobs would be performed by robots, while humans could focus more on creativity, social relationships, leisure and personal growth – perhaps ushering in an era of **abundance and shared well-being** made possible by intelligent automation. AI could also help **decision making process** public: through simulations and impartial analysis of enormous amounts of information, it could support governments and communities in making better decisions (for example on urban planning, health policies, pandemic management).

Fears and challenges: Conversely, many warn that without proper guidance, AI could lead to disturbing scenarios. One of them is the risk of a **superintelligence out of control** – often evoked by science fiction – whereby an AI far beyond the human level could escape our ability to manage. Although this scenario (the**AGI** – Artificial General Intelligence, and beyond, the so-called **technological singularity**) is speculative, some experts seriously discuss how to ensure that any superintelligent AI has values aligned with humans (*AI alignment problem*). Without going to extreme cases, there is already the danger today that very complex systems make decisions that we do not fully understand, with potentially negative consequences.

Another concrete fear is that of a **hyper-controlled world** and unequal. AI could give authoritarian governments unprecedented tools of surveillance and repression (such as the aforementioned facial recognition to follow dissidents, or social scoring systems to reward/punish behavior). If concentrated in the hands of a few (large companies or superpowers), AI could widen the power gap: technological elites would have a huge advantage over the rest of the population, undermining democratic principles. We imagine a future in which a few control AI infrastructures – they could, if they wanted, manipulate information on a global scale, or influence markets and governments in their favor. This makes it crucial that the **governance dell'IA** is inclusive and multilateral, and that AI is developed in a distributed way, avoiding monopolies.

Then there is the philosophical aspect: how it will change **human condition** live with increasingly intelligent machines? We will have to redefine the concept of work, of social value (if it is no longer necessarily linked to work), and even the concept of **consciousness** and **human uniqueness**. If one day robots or algorithms will be able to converse, create art, perhaps experience simulated emotions, how will we consider them? Objects, people, or a new category? Some envisage the recognition of **moral rights** for advanced AI, should they reach a form of sentience - a theoretical debate for now but which literature and cinema have often addressed.

In everyday life, we will also have to cultivate a healthy relationship with technology: avoid alienation (already today there is talk of dependence on algorithms, echo chambers, etc.), maintain the **critical spirit** in the age of information generated by AI (think of the problem of fake news created by increasingly sophisticated AI, such as deepfake videos indistinguishable from the real thing - this could undermine trust in the evidence and deliberately confuse public opinion).

The role of humanity: Ultimately, AI is a **amplifier** – of what we are and what we want. If our economic and political systems aim for the common good, AI will be able to amplify the common good; if they only aim for profit or control, AI could accentuate injustice and authoritarianism. This is why it is essential that civil society, governments, supranational institutions and AI developers themselves work together to **drive ethically** technological development. Documents such as the European Parliament resolution on the "right of robots", or United Nations initiatives (for example the UN Secretary General has proposed the creation of a global body to monitor the risks of advanced AI) go in this direction.

One of the recurring phrases is that AI should be "**human-centric**" – human-centered – and "trustworthy". This implies transparency, fairness, respect for rules and rights, involvement of different stakeholders in its development. Instead of letting a few technocrats determine the future, the**digital literacy** mass will have to increase, so that more people can understand and participate in choices on how to use these technologies.

It is likely that over the next 10 to 20 years we will

see AI further permeate every field: widespread autonomous transportation, increasingly capable personal assistants, perfect simultaneous translation between languages, tailor-made entertainment generated on the spot, and who knows what else. This will also impact the job market, perhaps making the idea of universal incomes or more free time a reality if productivity grows enormously. We may also face unprecedented crises (e.g. large-scale automated cyberattacks, AI election manipulation, etc.) that will require international cooperation to thwart.

In essence, the **role of AI in the future of humanity** will probably be that of a **powerful tool** – a tool that extends our cognitive capabilities just as the machines of the past extended their physical ones. Like any tool, the outcome depends on how we use it. It can help us build a more prosperous, equitable and sustainable world, or it can contribute to oppressive divisions and controls. There **responsibility is ours**. AI has no intentions in itself: it will reflect ours. It is therefore imperative that as a species we ask ourselves what values and goals we want to pursue, and program our machines accordingly.

Conclusion

Throughout this essay we have taken a journey through time and the social implications of technology. We started from the 90s - an era of slow but revolutionary computers for the time, mobile phones the size of bricks and the internet in its infancy - and we have arrived at the ultra-connected digital present, where very powerful devices and artificial intelligence permeate every aspect of daily life. We compared yesterday's hardware and software with today's, noting improvements of several orders of magnitude in performance and functionality, and a worldwide spread of technological access.

en.wikipedia.org

. This evolution, driven by exponential laws like Moore's

blog.adobe.com

, has changed the way we communicate, work, inform ourselves and entertain.

The center of attention was then placed on**Artificial intelligence**, which has gone from a curiosity for experts to a key factor of

transformation. We have seen how AI has achieved remarkable goals: from symbolic victories to chess and Go
ibm.com

wired.com
, to practical applications in medicine, finance, transport, up to generative AI capable of communicating and creating content. AI assists us on a daily basis today (often behind the scenes), but it also raises important questions. In the essay we analyzed the **benefits** that AI brings – greater efficiency, new services, decision support, potential economic growth – balancing them with the **criticality**: risk to employment, concentration of power, impacts on privacy, discriminatory bias, etc.

In scope **economic**, AI promises a leap in productivity and innovation, but it must be managed to avoid inequality and mass unemployment
imf.org

electroiq.com

. In the **Work**, AI can free us from burdensome tasks and create new professions, but it requires active training policies and protections for those affected by automation. On the front of **privacy**, AI amplifies surveillance and profiling capabilities: regulations such as the GDPR and privacy-by-design techniques will be crucial to protect personal data in an era of big data

edri.org

. We also explored how AI touches others **human rights**: freedom of expression (with algorithmic filters that decide what we see)

edri.org

, non-discrimination (with the danger of algorithmic bias)

edri.org

, right to a fair trial (if using AI in the judiciary), right to life and security (with autonomous weapons), among others. All of this highlights the need for an approach **ethical and regulatory** to AI: as a society we must set limits and guidelines so that technology respects human dignity.

Finally, looking at the **future**, we have recognized that AI will play an increasingly central role in the

destiny of humanity. We are *"on the brink of a revolution"* which brings with it both opportunities and risks
<u>imf.org</u>
. The decisions we make now – in terms of investments, laws, education, global collaboration – will determine whether AI will be one **tool of emancipation** or control, a driver of shared prosperity or a factor of division. There is an emerging consensus that they are useful **enlightened policies** per *"Safely harness the vast potential of AI for the benefit of humanity"*
<u>imf.org</u>
, as stated by the IMF. This includes engaging diverse voices (engineers, philosophers, citizens, legislators) in shaping the direction of innovation.

In conclusion, the technological parable from the 1990s to today teaches us that technical progress is extraordinarily fast - what appears insurmountable in one decade becomes obsolete in the next - but social and regulatory progress must keep pace. Artificial intelligence, in particular, represents the **transformative force** of our era: like electricity or the internet in the past, AI is redefining possibilities and boundaries. **It's up to us** ensure that this transformation is at the service of man. At stake is the type of society that we will hand down to our children: a society in which technology and humanism reinforce each other, or one in which the balance tips dangerously towards technology to the detriment of human values. Guided by the lessons of the past and a shared ethical vision, we can direct innovation towards scenarios in which AI helps build a more just, prosperous future that respects the freedom and rights of all.

Throughout this essay we have explored the evolution of technology and artificial intelligence, their foundations and operating principles, applications in numerous sectors and philosophical, regulatory and social implications. A picture emerges in which AI is not just a technology, but a **transformative phenomenon** which touches every aspect of civilization: economic, legal, ethical, existential. The potential benefits are enormous - better medical care, more efficient and sustainable economies, more comfortable lives, new frontiers of knowledge - but the responsibilities that loom are equally great: preventing abuse, ensuring fairness, protecting human dignity and autonomy.

A common thread is the need to maintain**man in the center**. Whether in the cooperative development of AI (human-in-the-loop), in the definition of regulations inspired by human rights, or in directing scientific research towards beneficial ends, it is imperative that artificial intelligence remains a tool and does not become the ultimate goal for which human values are sacrificed. As the UNESCO principles state, *"the protection of human rights and dignity is the cornerstone"* of every approach to AI
unesco.org

unesco.org
. This also means including different voices in the dialogue on AI: not only engineers and entrepreneurs, but jurists, philosophers, community representatives, women, minorities, developing countries - so that the AI of the future reflects the diversity and real needs of humanity.

From the comparison between utopian and

dystopian futuristic visions we have learned that the future is not written: it will depend on the choices we make today. We can work for **"Good" AI** – inclusive, fair, sustainable – through enlightened policies, education and responsible research. The risks (Orwellian surveillance, automated discrimination, mass unemployment, loss of control over overly powerful machines) are manageable if faced early and with international cooperation.

whitecase.com

whitecase.com

. It is important not to give in to either paralyzing technophobia or naive techno-optimism: it is needed **realism**.

Looking further, AI will perhaps force us to reconsider our very definition of intelligence and consciousness. It could make us rediscover the importance of unrepeatable human qualities (empathy, genuine creativity, wisdom) and stimulate us to cultivate them more. In an ideal scenario, the human-AI relationship will be of **virtuous complementarity**: AI will manage superhuman complexity, humans will instill vision, purpose and values. Together, they could tackle hitherto insoluble problems – from climate change to degenerative diseases – making progress that will benefit everyone.

Ultimately, **technology and humanity must not be in antithesis**, but allies. As in all previous revolutions, the direction we take will depend on how wisely we use our power. Artificial Intelligence amplifies our collective intelligence: it is up to us to use it to amplify it too **compassion** and the **justice** collective. The wise Camus wrote: *"True generosity towards the future consists in giving everything to the present"*. Here, generosity towards the future of AI means commitment now - in parliamentary chambers, in laboratories, in companies, in schools - to channel this extraordinary technology towards a future in which prosperity and human values advance hand in hand.

Sources:

- Bazzoli, F. (2019). *IT of the 1990s—we've come a long way, baby.* Health Data Management – Nostalgia tech anni '90 healthdatamanagement.com

  healthdatamanagement.com
  .

- Roser, M. (2022). *The brief history of artificial intelligence: the world has changed fast — what might be next?* Our World in Data – AI progress vs human capabilities ourworldindata.org
  .

- Georgieva, K. (2024). *AI Will Transform the Global Economy. Let's Make Sure It Benefits Humanity.* IMF Blog – Impacts of AI on productivity, work and inequalities imf.org

  imf.org
  .

- IMF Staff (2023). *Exposure of Jobs to AI: Concepts, Estimates and Comparisons*. – Data on % of jobs exposed to AI (40% global, 60% advanced countries)
  imf.org

  imf.org

  .

- Gallup (2025). *Americans Use AI in Everyday Products Without Realizing It*. – Study: 99% of Americans use AI unknowingly
  news.gallup.com

  news.gallup.com

  .

- Mazuma (2023). *The Evolution of Mobile Phones: A 30-Year Journey*. – 90s phone: calls/SMS only, monochrome screen
  mazumamobile.com

  .

- Adobe Blog (2022). *Fast-forward — comparing a 1980s supercomputer to the modern smartphone*. – Smartphone 5,000 times faster than Cray-2
  blog.adobe.com

; Moore's law
blog.adobe.com

.

⊠ Elon University (s.d.). *Imagining the Internet: Early 90s*. – Internet users: 45M (1996), 150M (1999), 407M (2000)
elon.edu

.

⊠ Wikipedia (2021). *Global Internet usage*. – 5 billion internet users (53% population) by 2021
en.wikipedia.org

.

⊠ IBM (s.d.). *Deep Blue*. – Deep Blue beats Kasparov, turning point 1997
ibm.com

.

⊠ IBM (s.d.). *Watson, Jeopardy! champion*. – Watson vince a Jeopardy!, salto nel NLP (2011)
ibm.com

ibm.com

.

⊠ Wired (2016). *AlphaGo wins historic Go*

contest. – AlphaGo beats Lee Sedol, AI milestone (2016)
wired.com
.

▢ Politico (2020). *How Cambridge Analytica used AI*. – Use of AI and big data to influence elections (CA case)
politico.eu

politico.eu
.

▢ Politico (2020). *London's live facial recognition rollout*. – Criticisms: risk of mass surveillance from facial recognition
politico.eu
.

▢ EDRi (2020). *UN Special Rapporteur report on AI & human rights*. – AI risks for freedom of expression (filter bubble)
edri.org
, privacy (profiling)
edri.org
, non-discrimination (algorithmic bias)
edri.org
.

- ElectroIQ (2024). *AI Replacing Jobs Statistics*.
  – Estimates: 300M jobs at risk by 2030 (Goldman)
  electroiq.com
  , 83M lost vs 69M created by 2027 (WEF)
  electroiq.com

  electroiq.com
  , 375M workers to be retrained (McKinsey)
  electroiq.com
  .

Considerations

Technology in the 90s vs today: a comparative look

The 1990s represent an era of transition to the modern digital world. In that decade the **IT and Internet revolution** was taking its first steps: personal computers gradually became more common in homes and offices, analog cell phones allowed only voice calls, and Internet access was via slow and noisy dial-up modems. In 1995, for example, only about **14% of US adults had access to the Internet**, often via modem at 28.8 kbps

pewresearch.org

. Most people had never heard of the "World Wide Web" – in a 1995 survey, 42% of Americans said they didn't know what the Internet was.

pewresearch.org

. At the time, connecting meant tying up the phone line and waiting minutes for simple texts or images to load. A typical 1993 modem transmitted data to just **14.4 kilobits per second**, i.e. approximately 0.014 Mbit/s

gwsmedia.com

. As a result, now mundane activities like video streaming were unthinkable: downloading a short movie could take hours.

Figure: A typical mobile phone from the 1990s. These devices allowed only essential calls and SMS, with monochrome displays and external antennas,

a far cry from the functionality of today's smartphones.
ansa.it

On the contrary, **Today** we live in a hyper-connected context. By approximately 2023 **63% of the world's population is online** ourworldindata.org
, thanks to the widespread diffusion of broadband and mobile Internet. Connection speeds have increased thousands of times: fiber optic networks and mobile 5G allow data to be downloaded at hundreds of megabits per second, making high-definition video conferencing, real-time movie streaming and advanced applications such as virtual reality possible. Even the **mobile telephony** has made giant strides: from the "basic" mobile phones of the 90s we have moved on to today's smartphones, which are basically powerful pocket computers connected to the network. In 1990, there were approximately 12 million mobile phones in the world; today there are over 5 billion active mobile devices, with a large part of them made up of smartphones with Internet access ansa.it

ansa.it
. At the time, people used paper maps to orient themselves, to listen to music they had walkmans or CDs, and to watch films you had to go to a video cassette shop; Today, GPS navigation apps, music streaming and on-demand video platforms have made these services immediately available everywhere. Work and study tools have also changed radically: in the 1990s, paper encyclopedias or CD-ROMs (such as Microsoft Encarta) were used for research, while today Wikipedia and search engines provide instant information; traditional mail and fax have been replaced by email and instant messaging; typewriters have given way to word processing software and shared clouds.

In summary, today's technology is compared to the 90s **more powerful, faster and pervasive**. The **digitalisation** it has affected every sector: communications, entertainment, commerce, finance, education, public administration. Operations that in 1995 required effort and time (such as developing photos, sending documents or looking for information in the library) are now carried out with a few taps on a smartphone screen. This transformation has improved the productivity and convenience of daily life, but it has also introduced a **dependence on digital infrastructures** and new risks (cybersecurity, information overload, etc.) that were absent or marginal in the 1990s. To fully understand how we got to this point, it is useful to retrace the key stages of technological evolution from the 1990s to today.

Technological evolution: from the foundations of the 90s to today's digital revolution

In the 1990s, what is often called the **digital revolution**, or the transition from analogue to digital technologies
it.wikipedia.org
. We can identify some fundamental changes that have occurred in this evolutionary path:

- ⬜ **Personal computers and widespread computing**: If in the 1980s the computer was the prerogative of a few enthusiasts or for specialist uses, in the 1990s the home PC became increasingly common. Operating systems with a graphical interface (Windows 95, Mac OS) make computers more accessible to the general public. Computing power follows Moore's law, doubling the number of transistors in microprocessors approximately every 18 to 24 months: as a result, computers at the end of the 1990s were dozens of times more powerful than those at the beginning of the decade.
  pc-outlet.it
  . For example, the Intel Pentium processor (1993) with a few tens of MHz clock paved the way for modern multi-gigahertz chips with billions of transistors. This growing computing power, combined with falling hardware costs, has made it possible to run increasingly complex applications on personal machines and has fostered the birth of thriving software industries.

- ⬜ **Internet and global connectivity**: The Internet, born as an academic and military network decades earlier, exploded among the public in the 1990s. The invention of the World Wide Web by Tim Berners-Lee (1989) and the introduction of the first browsers (such as Mosaic in 1993) made it possible to navigate between web pages with hypertext links, catalyzing the exponential growth of the network.
  pewresearch.org

. In 1990 there were only a few hundred thousand Internet users in the world; by 2000 global users had risen to approx **360 million**, and today they exceed 5 billion. From the **modem 56k** we moved to ADSL connections in the 2000s (hundreds of Kbps) and then to **fiber optic lines** and 4G/5G in the years 2010-2020 (tens or hundreds of Mbps). This enormous growth in capacity has made it possible to consume multimedia content on a large scale and the emergence of innovative services (from **streaming video** all'**global e-commerce**). At the same time, the phenomenon of **social media**: at the end of the 90s, platforms such as Geocities and the first forums were born; in the 2000s MySpace and Facebook inaugurated the era of large-scale social networks, transforming the way in which people communicate and get information.

- **Mobile telephony and device ubiquity**: In the 1990s the mobile phone went from a luxury object to a gradually more accessible device. Think of the famous Nokia or Motorola clamshell models at the end of the decade: still without mobile Internet, but already widespread for calls and SMS. The real turning point came in 2000 with the convergence between telephones and PDAs (smartphones): the iPhone (2007) and Android phones introduced touch screens, mobile web browsing and app stores. In a few years it **smartphone** it becomes a universal tool for communicating, working, photographing, geolocating, making payments and much more. Today, more than 80% of adults in developed countries own a smartphone, and there are over 6 billion mobile subscriptions globally. The consequence is that the **"always on" connectivity** and digital services accompany us wherever we go: from instant messaging to GPS navigation, from the use of social media to health monitoring via mobile sensors.

- **Digital media and entertainment**: The 1990s saw the transition from analogue physical media to digital content. Music migrated from vinyl and cassette tapes to (digital) audio CD and then to MP3 files shared over the Internet (Napster, 1999). Photography moved from film to the first digital cameras at the end of the decade. Video has experienced the transition from VHS to DVD (introduced in 1996) as a digital medium. These trends prepare the ground for **streaming**: YouTube (2005) inaugurates the era of user-generated online videos, Netflix and Spotify (late 2000s) bring films and music to streaming, almost completely eliminating physical media. This has revolutionized the cultural industries and the way we consume entertainment, making access to content immediate and personalized, but also challenging traditional business models (think of the decline of video stores or music stores).

- ☐ **Innovation and new tech companies**: In the 1990s, many companies destined to shape the technological landscape were born and grew. For example, **Microsoft** consolidates its position in software with Windows and Office, becoming one of the most capitalized companies in the world; **Apple**, after a difficult period, laid the foundations for the rebirth with iMac and then iPod; **Google** was founded in 1998 by introducing a revolutionary search engine; **Amazon** (founded 1994) started as an online bookstore and then diversified and led e-commerce; **Netflix** (1997) starts as DVD rental by mail; **IBM** shifts the focus from hardware to services; realities destined to disappear with the dot-com bubble (Pets.com, Altavista, etc.) are also born, whose rise and fall between 1998 and 2001 highlights the first excesses of the new digital economy. Entering the 2000s and 2010s, these companies and other new ones (Facebook in 2004, Twitter 2006, etc.) become global giants, concentrating enormous amounts of data and economic power, and serving as engines of continuous innovation in areas such as digital advertising, cloud computing, artificial intelligence.

In conclusion, from the mid-90s to today we have witnessed **epochal changes**: technology has become more **small, fast and economical** (advanced microelectronics), more **connected and interoperable** (global Internet standards), more **intelligent** (sophisticated software and algorithms) and more **widespread in every area of human life** (from science to medicine, from transport to social relations). This constitutes the terrain on which, in the last decade, Artificial Intelligence has blossomed as a driving force of the new wave of innovation. Understanding the current role of AI and what the future holds requires analyzing both its positive contributions and its critical issues, in light of this rapid technological evolution.

The rise of Artificial Intelligence: the role of AI today

Among all the technologies that have emerged in recent years, the**Artificial intelligence** is considered the most disruptive. AI generally refers to the ability of a machine or software to perform tasks that it would require **human intelligence**, how to learn from experience, reason, make decisions, recognize complex patterns, understand natural language. Although the field of AI has origins in the 1950s, it is only in the last decade that it has experienced a leap in quality, thanks to the convergence of **large amounts of data**, **high computing power** (e.g. parallel processors and cloud computing) e **new machine learning algorithms** (especially the *deep learning*). Today, AI has become a ubiquitous technology, often invisible but active behind the scenes in many everyday services and products.

Figure: Conceptual representation of Artificial Intelligence - AI today uses neural networks and advanced integrated circuits to process enormous quantities of data, "learning" to recognize patterns and make complex decisions autonomously.

Current applications of AI: Virtually every industry has started integrating AI solutions. Nello **smartphone** that we carry in our pockets, AI algorithms manage facial or fingerprint recognition for unlocking, optimize in-camera photo shots, include voice commands aimed at virtual assistants (*"Hey Siri"*, *"OK Google"*), translate texts in real time. On **Internet**, AI-powered recommendation systems suggest videos to watch, music tracks or products to buy based on our tastes (by analyzing huge datasets of user preferences). THE **social network** they use AI to filter content in the feed, recognize faces in photos, identify and remove inappropriate material (with variable effectiveness). In the'**industry and logistics**Intelligent robots and software automate assembly lines, manage warehouses by optimizing routes and times, and control product quality with artificial vision. In **medicine**, AI helps diagnose diseases by analyzing radiological images (e.g. algorithms that detect tumor nodules early in a CT scan) and assists in the discovery of new drugs by analyzing molecular data. In the **transport**, AI is the "brains" of self-driving vehicles and advanced driver assistance systems (ADAS), capable of recognizing road signs, pedestrians and other cars and making decisions in fractions of a second. Even in creative fields like**art and music**, generative algorithms (generative adversarial neural networks, GPT-type transformers, etc.) compose melodies, paint virtual pictures or write texts imitating human style.

This pervasive diffusion makes AI a technology **enabling** the *general purpose*, often compared to electricity due to the breadth of its applications. A clear sign of the growing importance of AI is its adoption in industry: according to a 2021 global survey, the **56% of companies have implemented AI in at least one function or process**
mckinsey.com
, up from 50% the previous year. The most common use cases include**optimization of service operations**, improving products with AI capabilities, contact center automation and predictive data analytics
mckinsey.com
. Cutting-edge businesses are already reporting a positive impact on profits: 27% of respondents in that study attributed at least a 5% increase in profits to AI.
mckinsey.com
. This shows that AI is not just laboratory experimentation, but one **concrete lever of economic value**. Governments and institutions are investing massively: the European Union, for example, through programs such as Horizon Europe and Digital Europe, has planned investments of around 1 billion euros per year in AI projects, with the aim of mobilizing a total of 20 billion euros per year together with private individuals.
digital-strategy.ec.europa.eu

digital-strategy.ec.europa.eu
. This race for AI is motivated by the belief that nations that can better develop and adopt artificial intelligence will have a competitive advantage

in terms of productivity, innovation and economic growth.

AI and everyday life: For the average user, many benefits of AI manifest themselves in more efficient and personalized services. For example, AI allows search engines to understand the intent behind user queries, providing more relevant results (even interpreting natural language questions). Email spam filters use intelligent algorithms to detect unwanted emails with very high accuracy. AI-powered digital maps can predict traffic and suggest alternative routes. In online stores, AI-powered chatbots answer common customer questions 24/7. "Smart home" devices use AI to adjust the optimal temperature by learning the habits of the occupants, or to recognize complex voice commands (turn on lights, play music, order groceries). All of this contributes to a **better user experience**, often without realizing that there is a machine learning algorithm behind it.

It should be emphasized that today's AI, while advanced, is generally a**"Restricted" AI (ANI)**, specialized in specific tasks. For example, a system that recognizes faces cannot drive a car, an algorithm that plays chess at a superhuman level cannot do linguistic translations. Every AI excels at one **strict dominion** thanks to targeted training and optimization data. The scope of the so-called **General AI (AGI)** – an artificial intelligence with general cognitive abilities comparable to those of humans – remains theoretical and the subject of research for now. However, progress is so rapid that many experts believe it is possible to achieve AGI this century cam.ac.uk

cam.ac.uk

. Organizations such as OpenAI, DeepMind and leading universities are continuously advancing the state of the art, demonstrated by milestones such as **AlphaGo** (the DeepMind program that in 2016 defeated the world champion of Go, a complex strategy game long considered out of reach for computers) and like the most recent **generative AI systems** capable of producing realistic text, images and even videos. These evolutions take us towards a future in which AI will be increasingly powerful and integrated into every aspect of society - a scenario that requires careful analysis **benefits** and **criticality** of this technology to prepare for its implications.

Benefits of AI in the economy and work

Artificial Intelligence is often referred to as the **new frontier of productivity**. By integrating AI into economic processes, companies can achieve significant efficiencies: automation of repetitive tasks, very rapid analysis of big data to support decisions, mass customization of products and services, reduction of human errors, optimization of the use of resources. All this translates into enormous potential macroeconomic benefits. An estimate from the consultancy firm PwC predicts that **by 2030, AI could contribute $15.7 trillion to the global economy**, with an increase in global GDP of 14%
weforum.org
. This impact would be greater than the current combined output of China and India – a measure of how AI can be a *"game changer"* for growth
weforum.org

weforum.org
. The greatest economic repercussions would come from both **improvement of work productivity** (thanks to automation and intelligent support for human operators) both from**increase in consumer demand** due to innovative products and services made possible by AI
weforum.org
.

In concrete terms, one of the most immediate benefits of AI in work is the**automation of repetitive, tiring or dangerous tasks**. In factories, robots equipped with intelligent vision and control can carry out assembly tasks around the clock without getting tired, freeing human workers from monotonous and strenuous tasks. In logistics warehouses, routing algorithms optimize the movement of goods by reducing downtime. In call centers, **virtual assistants** AI-based handle first-level customer requests (basic information, password reset, shipment tracking), allowing human operators to focus on more complex or valuable cases. In the banking and insurance sector, AI systems accelerate checks on transactions and practices (e.g. *robo-advisor* for investments, automatic evaluation of loan requests), increasing the speed of service. In agriculture, the **precision farming platforms** with AI they analyze weather and soil data to optimize irrigation and the use of fertilizers, reducing costs and environmental impact.

Another essential contribution is the **better data-driven decision-making ability** (*data-driven decision making*). Tools **machine learning** they can sift through huge amounts of business or market data to find hidden patterns and relationships not apparent to the human eye. For example, by analyzing sales data, customer reviews and social trends, an algorithm can help a company predict demand for a product with greater accuracy, thus optimizing inventories (reducing both stock outs and waste of unsold items). Or, by cross-referencing financial, operational parameters and news, AI can support managers in identifying emerging risks or investment opportunities. On the stock exchange, the majority of trading operations are already carried out by high-frequency automatic algorithms; tomorrow, more sophisticated AI could manage portfolios adaptively, reacting to weak signals much earlier than human managers.

AI can too **create new jobs and new markets**. Each technological wave has historically generated both the destruction of obsolete occupations and the creation of new professions. In the case of AI, alongside the decline of some manual or administrative roles, we are seeing the birth of figures like the **data scientist**, l'**machine learning engineer**, l'**expert in AI ethics**, The **AI systems trainer** (for example training chatbots), roles that were unthinkable until a few years ago. According to the *World Economic Forum*, within the next few years AI and automation could eliminate millions of traditional jobs but at the same time generate new ones - with a potentially positive balance, as long as the workforce is retrained. An OECD report found that approximately **32% of jobs will experience significant changes** in jobs due to automation, but many workers will be able to evolve towards tasks complementary to AI instead of being replaced
thinkdigitalpartners.com
. The key is training: AI can take on repetitive tasks, but human skills in creativity, critical thinking, management, communication will remain valuable and will need to be enhanced in combination with intelligent tools.

Finally, AI offers benefits in solving complex problems on a social scale:

optimizing energy consumption in cities (smart grids managed by AI that reduce waste), improving urban traffic planning (reducing congestion and pollution), accelerating scientific research (e.g. DeepMind's AI which solved the problem of protein folding with AlphaFold, helping the biomedical sector). These advancements can translate into **sustainable economic growth** and progress in collective well-being. In summary, AI acts as **innovation engine**: enables previously impossible products and services, increases efficiency and quality in many processes, and acts as a multiplier of human productivity. However, along with these benefits, significant critical issues also emerge, especially regarding the effects on the world of work and the possible resulting inequalities.

Critical issues for work and the economy: Intelligent automation, if not accompanied by adequate measures, can lead to **loss of jobs** in different sectors. Low-skilled workers or those who carry out routine tasks are the most exposed to the risk of replacement by automated systems. Initial studies had predicted alarming scenarios: a famous 2013 Oxford study (Frey and Osborne) estimated that 47% of jobs in the United States were at risk of automation within one to two decades.
thinkdigitalpartners.com
. More recent estimates are less drastic – for example, the OECD in 2018 downsized the share of occupations at high risk of automation to **14% in advanced countries**, with a further 32% of jobs that will undergo significant transformations
thinkdigitalpartners.com

thinkdigitalpartners.com
– but they agree that millions of workers will have to adapt to new jobs. In absolute numbers, that 14% in the OECD area corresponds to approximately **66 million jobs potentially eliminated**
thinkdigitalpartners.com
. The manufacturing, logistics, transportation sectors (think self-driving trucks that could one day reduce the need for drivers) and some routine services (bank branches, secretariats) are among the most vulnerable.

This perspective generates understandable **social anxieties**: there is the fear of a *"jobless society"*, a society with less human labor available. While technology has historically created more jobs than it has destroyed, the pace of AI raises the question of whether this time the change risks being too rapid for the job market to adapt to it painlessly. Some economists warn that without interventions there could be an increase in **economic inequality**: the benefits of automation could focus on capital and high skills (engineers, technology owners), while replaced workers could struggle to reintegrate. Furthermore, the bargaining power of labor could decrease in sectors where the automatic alternative becomes credible, compressing wages and protections. These dynamics require active policies: **professional retraining**, continuous education to acquire digital skills, support for job mobility towards growth sectors, and perhaps the idea of measures such as a **universal basic income** returns to the debate as a safety net in a future with unstable employment.

Another problem is that measuring productivity gains from AI is not straightforward. Implementing effective AI systems requires investments, infrastructure, skills and even a rethink of business processes. Not all companies, especially SMEs, have the resources to do it immediately, risking creating a **gap** between companies (and nations) at the forefront of AI and others that lag behind. This technological gap can translate into **market concentration**: large tech companies, already dominant today, can further expand their competitive advantage thanks to AI (having access to more data and better talent). There is therefore the danger of less competitive markets and the emergence of global AI oligopolies. Institutions are called to avoid these outcomes through antitrust updated for the digital age and by encouraging the democratic diffusion of innovations (open source, startup ecosystems, etc.).

In summary, AI offers substantial economic benefits – increased production, new goods and services, long-term growth – but poses immediate challenges for workers and for the fair distribution of the fruits of this growth. As noted by **World Economic Forum**, "it's not true that robots will steal all our work, but the tasks will change" and we need to prepare ourselves with adequate policies
it.wikipedia.org

it.wikipedia.org

. A guided and inclusive transition can ensure that AI translates into widespread prosperity; vice versa, ignoring critical issues could amplify social disparities and tensions. In the next chapter we will address another crucial aspect: the impact of AI on privacy and human rights, which represents a different order of challenges compared to economic ones.

Impacts of AI on privacy and human rights

The era of Big Data and AI raises pressing questions about **privacy** of individuals and on respect for **fundamental rights**. In fact, AI applications often require large amounts of data to "learn" and make accurate decisions. This data can include sensitive personal information: from our online habits tracked for advertising purposes, to facial images collected by surveillance cameras, to health data used for predictive models. While on the one hand the ability of AI to analyze such data brings benefits (personalized services, security, early medical diagnoses, etc.), on the other hand it opens the door to potential abuses and violations of the private sphere and people's rights.

Surveillance and misuse of data: An emblematic case is that of **surveillance via facial recognition**. Today, AI-enhanced smart cameras can identify faces in real time within video streams by comparing them to image databases. This can help locate criminals or missing persons, but in the hands of authoritarian governments or unscrupulous private actors it can turn into a **pervasive control system**. In some Chinese cities, for example, the combination of ubiquitous cameras and facial recognition software fuels the so-called *social credit system*, where citizens' behavior is monitored and evaluated, raising serious ethical concerns in the West. Even in liberal democracies, the indiscriminate use of mass surveillance technologies risks eroding constitutional rights such as **freedom of movement and anonymity** in public space. For this reason, civil rights organizations are calling for moratoriums or bans on these practices. In 2021, the UN High Commissioner for Human Rights Michelle Bachelet called for a **global moratorium on the use of AI systems at high risk to human rights**, in particular on remote biometric recognition in public spaces, given the threat it poses to fundamental freedoms
media.un.org
. He clearly stated that **some AI applications that cannot be used in compliance with international human rights law should be banned**
media.un.org

media.un.org
.

In addition to visual surveillance, there is the question of **personal data online**. Each of our digital interactions - searches, clicks, purchases, posts on social media - generates traces that AI algorithms aggregate and analyze. Technology and advertising companies profile billions of users to predict their behavior and target targeted advertising. This economic model, although legitimate within certain limits, can easily lead to **privacy violations** if there is a lack of transparency and informed consent. The Cambridge Analytica scandal (2018) showed how the data of millions of Facebook users was collected without permission and used by algorithms to influence electoral campaigns, highlighting the risks for **democracy** itself when AI is used to manipulate public opinion through propagandistic micro-targeting. In general, AI allows for such sophisticated analysis to make inferences **sensitive information** even from apparently harmless data: for example, by analyzing "likes" on social media, a model can most likely guess a person's political orientation or ethnicity; through geolocation data and daily activities, religious habits or health conditions can be deduced. This poses a serious problem **protection of personal identity**.

Algorithmic bias and discrimination: Another impact on human rights arises from the fact that AI algorithms can inherit – or even amplify – biases present in the data with which they are trained. If a system of *machine learning* is trained on historical data to make decisions (e.g. selecting candidates for a job, granting a loan, assessing a prisoner's risk of recidivism), and that data reflects disparities or biases (conscious or unconscious) in society, the AI will tend to replicate them. Concrete cases have caused a stir: algorithms **personnel selection** used by large companies have penalized female candidates because they were trained on historical data in which male hires prevailed; systems **credit scoring** automated systems have offered worse conditions to ethnic minorities with the same creditworthiness, reflecting previous disparities; predictive software for criminal justice in the USA (e.g. COMPAS) have been accused of assigning higher risk scores to black defendants than to white defendants, given the same background - with the risk of discrimination in the granting of bail.

media.un.org

. These examples show how AI, if not carefully designed and monitored, can undermine the principle of **equality** and the right to a **fair treatment**. The **EU Charter of Fundamental Rights** and many national constitutions prohibit discrimination based on gender, race, religion, orientation, etc.; however, an "opaque" algorithm could introduce de facto differentiated treatments, which are difficult to identify and contest because they are masked behind apparent mathematical neutralities. This raises the crucial issue of **transparency and accountability** of algorithms (which we will talk about in the ethics section): citizens should have the right to know when a significant decision is made by an AI and to obtain understandable explanations, as well as the possibility of appeal.

Threat to autonomy and dignity: Ubiquitous AI can also impact more intangible rights such as **personal autonomy** and the **freedom of thought**. Extreme personalization algorithms, which only show us content "tailored" to our preferences, risk locking us in **bowl informative** and direct our choices without us realizing it. Furthermore, techniques **algorithmic manipulation** – for example notifications designed to create addiction, *dark pattern* in interfaces that induce certain clicks, or even *deepfake* realistic used to spread misinformation - can influence opinions and behaviour, endangering the right to freely form thoughts. The UN has warned that AI systems designed to manipulate human behavior (e.g. exploiting psychological vulnerabilities for commercial or political purposes) are contrary to respect for dignity and should be prohibited. digital-strategy.ec.europa.eu
. The **human dignity**, the cornerstone of all rights, could also be harmed by degrading AI applications: think of social systems that spread automatically generated hate speech or behavioral scoring that labels people as "reliable" or "unreliable" on arbitrary grounds. Fortunately, there is growing awareness of these risks and work to mitigate them through ethical and regulatory guidelines (reviewed in the next sections).

The right to privacy as a fundamental right: Privacy is not just a quirk, but a recognized human right (art. 12 Universal Declaration of Human Rights, art. 8 European Convention on Human Rights, art. 17 UN Covenant on Civil and Political Rights). It guarantees it **space of personal freedom** within which to develop one's individuality without surveillance or arbitrary interference. AI, with its intrusion capabilities, puts pressure on this space.

In Europe, the **General Data Protection Regulation (GDPR)** since 2018 it has tried to stem these risks by imposing principles of **data limitation, clear goals, explicit consent** and recognizing the right not to be subjected to decisions based solely on automated processing if they have significant legal effects on the person (art. 22 GDPR). However, the practical application is complex: users often give up their data without full knowledge in exchange for "free" services, and controls on the internal operation of big tech algorithms are difficult. Precisely for this reason, guarantee figures such as the Privacy Guarantors and international bodies are asking for greater **transparency** and possibility of **audit** independent on AI systems, to verify compliance with rights.

In conclusion, AI greatly amplifies the ability to collect and analyze information about people, which can collide with privacy, freedom and equality. Without adequate safeguards, we risk an Orwellian "Big Brother" society, in which every action is monitored, or a society in which **unfair automated decisions** they affect vulnerable subjects without them even understanding why. These negative scenarios are not inevitable: on the contrary, they are at the center of the current ethical and regulatory debate, which aims to **guide the development of AI in a way that preserves human rights**. The next section will be dedicated to the ethical and social aspects, where we will see how the scientific community, institutions and public opinion are facing these challenges.

Ethical and social aspects of the diffusion of AI

The large-scale development and adoption of artificial intelligence raises **profound ethical questions**. Unlike past technologies, AI makes decisions (or recommendations) that affect human beings, often in a way that is not directly controllable or understandable by its creators (the phenomenon of "*black box*"). It therefore becomes crucial to ensure that these systems respect shared moral principles and values. The main ethical and social aspects under discussion include: **transparency, equity and non-discrimination, accountability, safety, beneficence vs maleficence, human autonomy** and **overall social impact**.

Transparency and explainability: One of the key principles is that AI should operate in a transparent way, that is, understandable and explainable to humans. This does not mean revealing source code or trade secrets, but providing **meaningful explanations** on the functioning and decision-making criteria of algorithms, especially when they affect the rights of individuals. For example, if an AI system refuses a mortgage or selects candidates for a job, the person involved should be able to know for what reasons (determining factors) this happened, instead of just receiving an enigmatic "automatic outcome". There **explainability** it is also important to allow independent verification and correct any errors or biases. However, many modern AIs, especially the **deep neural networks**, are opaque by nature: they learn complex internal parameters that have no immediate meaning for humans. The research on "**AI interpretability**" tries precisely to extract reasoning or highlight the parts of the data to which the neural network pays attention during a decision, to give humans back a certain cognitive control over the system. From an ethical point of view, transparency is linked to **right to explanation** of the user and the principle of honesty: an AI should not deliberately deceive the user about its nature (hence also the recommendation that it is always clear when interacting with a machine and not with a person, to avoid fraud or confusion
digital-strategy.ec.europa.eu
).

Equity, bias and inclusiveness: As discussed, there is a risk that AI perpetuates or amplifies discriminatory biases. Therefore AI ethics imposes a strong imperative to **equity** (*fairness*): systems must be designed and trained to avoid illicit bias towards protected groups (women, ethnic, religious, LGBTQ+ minorities, disabled people, etc.). This requires balanced datasets, techniques to mitigate bias (e.g. equalizing results between groups, if warranted), and a testing phase that evaluates outputs with fairness metrics. The principle of **non-discrimination** is also reiterated at a policy level: the European ethical guidelines speak of **"diversity, non-discrimination and fairness"** as key requirements, underlining that AI must not marginalize vulnerable groups and indeed should be accessible to all
digital-strategy.ec.europa.eu

digital-strategy.ec.europa.eu
. Including diverse perspectives in development (e.g. diverse development teams, engaging stakeholders and impacted communities) is considered a good practice to avoid "groupthink" that overlooks categories of people. In addition to social justice, there is also a pragmatic argument: fair, bias-free AI is also more accurate and robust, while biased AI can make suboptimal decisions (e.g., overlooking qualified candidates just because they come from a certain background).

Accountability and responsibility: If an AI system causes damage or an error, who is responsible? This is an open question in the ethical and legal debate. The principle of **accountability** implies that there must always be a clear attribution of responsibility to human subjects – developers, producers, users – for the actions of an AI
digital-strategy.ec.europa.eu
. It is not acceptable to place the blame on a machine as if it were an autonomous entity beyond any control. This has practical implications: systems should be **audible**, i.e. subject to verification (via logs, documentation, monitoring) to determine what went wrong and prevent recurrences
digital-strategy.ec.europa.eu
. Furthermore, there should be a **appeal and redress mechanism**: If an individual is wronged by an algorithmic decision, they must be able to ask

for human review and obtain remedy (for example, correction of the wrong decision, or compensation if there is damage). At a social level, the question of responsibility also affects the regulatory framework: legislators are thinking about how to adapt laws on civil and criminal liability to the use of AI (for example, in autonomous vehicles: is the software manufacturer, the owner of the vehicle, the passenger, all of them in competition responsible?). The EU is working on a **AI Liability Act** complementary to the IA Regulation to clarify these points
digital-strategy.ec.europa.eu

digital-strategy.ec.europa.eu
.

Beneficence and non-maleficence: In the context of AI, the bioethical principle of "doing good and avoiding evil" translates into the idea that AI must be designed to **maximize human well-being and minimize risks**. A concept introduced by the EU guidelines is that of **"Societal and environmental well-being"**: systems should bring benefits to all human beings, including future generations, and be sustainable and sensitive to environmental impact
digital-strategy.ec.europa.eu
. This means considering, for example, long-term effects on the social fabric and cohesion when introducing new AI technology (avoiding applications that may deliberately cause social harm). It also means evaluating the ecological footprint: training the most complex AI models consumes enormous amounts of energy; an ethical use of AI requires balancing progress with environmental protection, perhaps favoring more efficient models or offsetting emissions. The principle of non-maleficence implies above all attention to **safety**: AI must be **robust and reliable** to avoid causing unintentional damage. For example, in the healthcare sector, an AI diagnostic system must be carefully validated to avoid making errors that compromise the health of patients; In transportation, an autonomous car must meet rigorous safety standards to avoid accidents. The requirements of **technical robustness** include the ability to manage unexpected cases, to resist attacks (e.g. *adversarial examples* which confuse artificial vision), to fail in a controlled manner (emergency mode with human intervention)

digital-strategy.ec.europa.eu

. Develop an AI **safe** it is first of all an ethical imperative towards the users who will rely on it.

Human autonomy and control: A recurring theme is how to maintain**man "in the circuit"** decision-making. The guidelines talk about *"Human agency and oversight"*: AI should **enhance** human beings, not completely replace them in decisions, and human supervision mechanisms must be guaranteed

digital-strategy.ec.europa.eu

. There are various models: *human-in-the-loop* (the human approves every critical decision proposed by the AI), *human-on-the-loop* (the human intervenes only in case of malfunction, monitoring from outside), *human-in-command* (human can cancel or turn off the system at any time)

digital-strategy.ec.europa.eu

. The choice depends on the context, but in sensitive domains – think of justice, health, weapons – there is consensus that an element of **significant human control** is necessary to respect the dignity and freedom of the individuals involved. The concern is to avoid a scenario of *"automation in the dark"* where people become passive executors of what the machine says. This would closely link AI ethics with democratic principles: not blindly delegating vital decision-making powers to non-human entities, especially if there is no social consensus on this. The case of **lethal autonomous weapons** (*"killer robots"*): the possibility of drones or weapon systems identifying and engaging targets without human supervision poses a serious ethical dilemma. A broad coalition of scientists and activists is calling for a pre-emptive international ban to ensure that **life-or-death decisions remain under direct human control**, in line with humanitarian law (principle of responsibility and humanity in armed conflict). Several countries support this initiative, although at the moment there is not yet a binding treaty – the discussion continues in the UN.

Social impact and common good: The massive introduction of AI can alter social balances: for example, the**employment** (discussed before) but also the**human interaction**. If many relationship and care functions were carried out by machines (think of robot carers for the elderly, or bots that keep lonely people company), what would be the consequences on community bonds? There is a risk of one **dehumanization** of certain relationships if you rely too much on impersonal artificial intelligence. Another aspect is the possible **digital divide**: AI could benefit those who have access to technologies and penalize those who are excluded (due to economic, geographical or generational conditions). Guarantee a**Inclusive AI** it means working so that the benefits are shared and do not increase inequalities. For example, if AI improves diagnostic healthcare, it is necessary to ensure that these tools are available not only in richer hospitals but also in less developed contexts, otherwise innovation widens health gaps. Similarly in education: AI can personalize learning, but if only some elite schools can afford advanced AI tutors, there is a risk of accentuating the educational gap.

To address all these issues, numerous institutions have produced **codes of ethics and guidelines**. In addition to the aforementioned ethical guidelines of the European Commission (2019) which identify **7 requirements for trustworthy AI** – from respect for fundamental rights to technical robustness
digital-strategy.ec.europa.eu

digital-strategy.ec.europa.eu

digital-strategy.ec.europa.eu
– i. should be mentioned **OECD Principles on AI (2019)**, signed by many countries, which affirm among other things: inclusive and sustainable growth, human values and primary rights, transparency, robustness and accountability
consilium-europa.libguides.com
. Even the**UNESCO** in 2021 it adopted a Recommendation on the ethics of AI, the first global regulatory instrument on the topic, which lists values (respect for dignity, the environment, diversity) and actions (ethical impact assessments, promotion of digital literacy, data governance) to be implemented. AI ethics committees have been created in academia and industry, and big tech companies such as Google have drawn up their own AI Principles, committing themselves not to develop technologies that are contrary to human rights or aimed at illegitimate surveillance.

Naturally, ethical guidelines alone are not enough: they must be translated into concrete practices and, often, into binding regulations. This is where regulatory efforts come into play, the topic of the next chapter, where we will see how the legislator is trying to transform these principles into implementing rules so that the development of AI occurs within **safe tracks that respect social values**.

AI laws and regulations

As AI pervades critical tasks, governments are taking action **regulate their use** and prevent unwanted effects. We are still at the beginning of this journey: unlike traditional sectors such as pharmaceuticals or transport, AI did not have a dedicated regulatory framework until recently. However, technological acceleration has convinced many jurisdictions of the need to set clear rules of the game. The goal is **maximize the benefits of AI while protecting safety, rights and ethical principles**. This is a delicate balance: excessive regulation could stifle innovation, but the lack of rules risks leaving dangerous gaps.

The European Union at the forefront: The EU is taking a pioneering role with what is often called the world's first comprehensive AI law proposal: the **Artificial Intelligence Regulation (AI Act)**. Presented by the European Commission in April 2021
digital-strategy.ec.europa.eu
, the AI Act adopts an approach based on **risk**: defines categories of AI use based on the level of risk they present to fundamental rights, security and values, and imposes obligations proportionate to those risks
digital-strategy.ec.europa.eu

digital-strategy.ec.europa.eu
. In particular:

- ☐ **Little to no risk**: Many AI applications (e.g. video games, anti-spam filters) are considered low risk and do not meet specific additional requirements. The EU leaves them free to develop, but encourages voluntary codes of conduct.

- ☐ **Limited risk**: Some systems only require transparency obligations. For example, the *deepfake* (synthetic content generated by AI that appears real) will have to be clearly labeled as artificial artifacts, so as not to deceive users
digital-strategy.ec.europa.eu
. Chatbots also have to claim that they are not human when interacting with people. These measures aim to inform the user and mitigate risks of manipulation.

- ☐ **High risk**: It is the most important category. It includes AI systems used in critical contexts such as: security (e.g. algorithms that decide whether to arrest a person), essential infrastructures (transport, energy), education (software that evaluates students), employment (recruiting or employee management software), financial services (credit scoring), migration and border control, healthcare (diagnostics), and other areas in which an error or bias can seriously harm rights or safety. For these systems the AI Act provides stringent requirements: **risk and compliance assessment** before placing on the market, quality obligations of training data (to reduce bias), detailed technical documentation, traceability of results, creation of event logs, transparency towards users, post-market surveillance and possibility of independent audits artificialintelligenceact.eu

  digital-strategy.ec.europa.eu
  . Suppliers will have to register these systems in a dedicated EU database. In practice, a "high risk" AI will have to pass a sort of "certification" before it can be used - similarly to what happens with medical devices or machinery, but applied to software.

- ☐ **Unacceptable risk (prohibited)**: The EU intends to ban some AI applications deemed to be against European values. According to the proposal, they would be **prohibited**: the systems of **social scoring** generalized by governments (assessing the social trustworthiness of people on a large scale, China style) digital-strategy.ec.europa.eu
  ; the systems they implement **subliminal manipulation or exploit vulnerabilities** of specific groups to alter their behavior in a harmful way (for example AI toys that encourage minors to carry out dangerous acts) digital-strategy.ec.europa.eu
  ; and in general the**use of "real-time" facial recognition in public spaces for legal purposes** (except for very narrow exceptions for serious threats, and in any case with judicial authorization) digital-strategy.ec.europa.eu
  . This last point has been the subject of debate: the European

Parliament is pushing for an almost total ban on public facial recognition, while some member states would like exceptions for national security. In any case, the orientation is to prohibit those AI practices that result **incompatible with fundamental rights** – such as dignity, privacy, non-discrimination, freedom – or with democratic principles (e.g. indiscriminate mass surveillance). This sets an important precedent: not every innovation is acceptable, there are some that the company chooses not to implement.

The AI Act, after consultations and legislative process, reached a political agreement at the end of 2023
digital-strategy.ec.europa.eu
. It is expected to enter into force in 2024, but with effective application after a transitional period (perhaps in 2025/2026)
digital-strategy.ec.europa.eu
. It will be the first example of **complete regulatory framework on AI**: not a generic ban nor total laissez-faire, but **punctual rules** for developers, distributors and users of AI systems. For example, a company that wants to market AI medical diagnosis software (high risk) in Europe will have to comply with the technical requirements and get certified; a municipality intending to use a continuous facial recognition system for urban security would find that this is prohibited; a social platform that uses deepfakes will have to label them. The Commission's hope is twofold: to protect citizens and at the same time **create trust** towards AI, also stimulating its adoption (because users and businesses trust regulated and safe technology more)
digital-strategy.ec.europa.eu
. Furthermore, the EU aspires to **shape global standards** ("gold standard") on the subject, as already done with privacy through the GDPR
digital-strategy.ec.europa.eu
. In fact, it is likely that other countries will adapt their practices to be able to interface with the European market (Brussels effect).

Other jurisdictions and global initiatives: In the rest of the world, the regulatory landscape is evolving. There **China** has issued specific guidelines and regulations on aspects of AI, such as the rules on deepfakes (which require reporting them) and the recommendation algorithm (which impose transparency on the recommendation algorithms of online platforms). However, the Chinese approach is different: it emphasizes state control and censorship of content deemed destabilizing, rather than the protection of individual privacy. **United States**: At the federal level there is no omnibus law on AI (yet). There has been more focus on industry self-regulation approaches and non-binding guidelines: for example, in 2020 the Institute of Electrical and Electronics Engineers (IEEE) published ethical standards for the design of autonomous systems (**IEEE Ethically Aligned Design**), and in October 2022 the White House released a document called "**AI Bill of Rights**" (Blueprint for an AI Bill of Rights) which lists principles to protect citizens – such as secure systems, protection from algorithmic discrimination, data privacy, transparency, humane alternatives – but it is precisely a **charter of principles** without immediate force of law. However, some individual US states have legislated: for example, Illinois has a law regulating the use of AI in video hiring interviews (requires consent and notification). Furthermore, in the USA several cities (San Francisco, Boston, Portland) have **the use of facial recognition is prohibited** by local law enforcement agencies, effectively anticipating the EU on this point, due to fears of error and racial profiling.

At an international level, in addition to the OECD and UNESCO already mentioned, the **G20** and the **G7** discussed common guidelines on AI. The G7 launched the partnership in 2018 **Global Partnership on AI (GPAI)** to encourage cooperation on these issues between democratic countries. The **United Nations** are considering the creation of a coordinating body on AI (some have proposed a sort of *IPCC for AI*, on the model of the climate panel). In the UN context, the most advanced discussion is perhaps that on **autonomous weapons** in the context of the Convention on Conventional Weapons (CCW), where, however, unanimous consensus on a ban is still lacking: military powers such as the USA, Russia, China are cautious in binding themselves, while over 30 countries (and global civil society) support the adoption of a treaty that maintains "significant human control" over weapons systems.

Regulate without stifling innovation: A widespread concern is how to reconcile rules and technological development. Too rigid or premature rules could prevent startups and researchers from experimenting and

competing in a rapidly evolving field. On the other hand, the absence of rules risks leading to sensational incidents that would undermine public trust. Policy makers are trying to calibrate interventions. The EU risk-based approach is appreciated because **targeted**: we intervene only where necessary (e.g. targeted bans on highly problematic uses and requirements only for sensitive sectors). Furthermore, the EU foresees **regulatory sandboxes**, controlled environments where companies can test innovative AI solutions in temporary derogation from some rules, under the supervision of the authorities, so as not to block innovation but evaluate its effects before a full launch
digital-strategy.ec.europa.eu
. Another key is to involve the industry in the definition of **technical standards**: many issues (e.g. how to document an AI model, how to verify bias, how to implement explainability) can be addressed with shared standards, so that compliance becomes common practice and not an excessive burden.

Ultimately, AI regulation is a new and evolving field. The regulatory framework will likely refine over time as we better understand the technology and its impacts. It is likely that in the coming years we will also see jurisprudence emerge from the courts on cases of liability, algorithmic discrimination, etc., which will help further clarify the boundaries. The important thing is that legislators proceed guided by the principle of **primacy of man over technology**: AI must serve society, operate within democratically established boundaries and not place itself above the law. In this sense, attention to regulation is in itself a sign of maturity in the approach to AI: we recognize its power and at the same time the need to channel it appropriately.

After exploring the benefits, risks and rules of AI, we are left to ask ourselves: **What future awaits us with AI increasingly present?** The final section will analyze the prospects for humanity, between extraordinary possibilities and caution on the most distant scenarios, to finally conclude our reflection.

Future prospects and possible implications

for humanity

Imagining the future of artificial intelligence means dealing with a spectrum of scenarios ranging from utopian to dystopian. On the one hand, there is the optimistic vision in which AI helps solve many of humanity's great challenges – disease, hunger, climate change, universal education – ushering in an era of prosperity and widespread knowledge. On the other hand, there is the fear that an AI that is out of control or used irresponsibly could aggravate inequalities, erode freedoms or even put the very survival of human civilization at risk. Experts often point out that the **future of AI is not predetermined**, but it depends on the choices we make today in terms of research, ethics and governance. So let's try to outline some perspectives:

AI as a tool for the common good: In a positive scenario, AI will become a **powerful ally of man** in dealing with complex problems. In medicine, by combining genomics, clinical data and predictive models, AI could enormously accelerate the development of personalized treatments for currently incurable diseases (think of the progress already glimpsed with AlphaFold in biology). In the fight against climate change, AI could optimize the management of energy networks, improve extreme weather forecasts, design low-emission materials and industrial processes. In agriculture, advanced algorithms will drive automated vertical farms and regenerative crops that feed growing populations while reducing ecological footprints. In the educational field, *tutor* Smart virtual schools could offer every student high-quality, personalized teaching, bridging the gap between those who have access to the best schools and those who don't. Many dangerous tasks – from defusing bombs to cleaning contaminated sites – could be carried out entirely by machines, saving lives. AI could also free up people's time by automating burdensome jobs and allowing society to focus more on creative, scientific, care and leisure activities. Some futurists outline the prospect of a "**age of abundance**" in which, thanks to intelligent automation, essential goods and services become very cheap and accessible, reducing extreme poverty. In essence, responsibly developed and democratized AI can amplify human ingenuity and accelerate progress on all fronts, potentially realizing many of the UN Sustainable Development Goals (health, education, zero hunger, clean water, etc.).

Towards a superintelligence? One of the most debated long-term issues is the possibility ofGeneral AI (AGI) and beyond, the **superintelligence** – an artificial intelligence that significantly surpasses human cognitive capabilities in almost all domains. Some experts (like Ray Kurzweil) predict that by the mid-21st century we could reach a technological "singularity": the moment when AI equals and then surpasses human intellect, triggering an acceleration beyond our control. If this happened, the implications would be immense. A benevolent superintelligence could help solve seemingly intractable problems and usher in an era of nearly limitless knowledge. However, a superintelligence that is poorly aligned with our values could behave in unpredictable or dangerous ways.
Stephen Hawking, reflecting on this scenario, warned that *"The creation of powerful AI could be the greatest event in the history of our civilization, but also the last, unless we learn to avoid the risks"*
cam.ac.uk
. He and other scientists emphasized the need for **prepare now** to manage entities that are more intelligent than us. In fact, organizations like the **Future of Life Institute** and the **Center for AI Safety** they study techniques for "**AI alignment**" (AI alignment), or how to ensure that advanced AI continues to pursue objectives beneficial to humanity and can be controlled even when its logical capabilities exceed ours. This includes concepts such as "invariant values", safety switches ("big red buttons"), simulations and rigorous testing before deploying a more intelligent system. Not all scholars agree that superintelligence is imminent; there are those who consider it science fiction or at least many decades away. But the general consensus is that **think ahead** these extreme outcomes are appropriate, because the stakes are incredibly high.

Long-term socio-economic impact: Whether or not strong AGI is achieved, over the next 10 to 20 years we will see AI further transform the economy and jobs. It is possible that many routine office jobs will disappear, while new roles will emerge. Some visionaries paint a future in which traditional human work is greatly reduced and society must reorganize itself around new models – for example, universal income systems or economies oriented towards creativity, assistance, experience. AI could also change the very concept of knowledge production: with systems capable of generating scientific theories or engineering projects, humans could move towards the role of supervisor and validator rather than direct creator. This opens up philosophical questions about what this will mean **be human** in a world where machines excel at many intellectual tasks: should we redefine our purpose by focusing on what machines cannot (yet) do, such as genuine empathy, moral intuition, art that communicates lived experience? There are those who see this as an opportunity for a sort of **human renaissance**, with more people dedicated to research, art, relationships, while material needs are largely satisfied by machines. Others, however, fear a crisis of meaning and identity for many, if work - a traditional source of dignity - were to disappear without an adequate replacement.

Dystopian and security risks: AI also brings threats that must be kept under control so that they do not compromise the future. One is the **autonomous arms race**: if an unregulated competition were to break out between powers to develop increasingly lethal and faster AI weapons, it could lead to an unstable situation (similar to the nuclear race) with enormous risks in the event of an error or accident. An armed drone that automatically acquires targets in microseconds can escape classic human "dual control," increasing the likelihood of accidental escalations. Another risk is the **digital authoritarianism**: Dictatorial regimes could consolidate unprecedented power by using AI to surveil and repress any dissent (we already see signs in this direction with current technology). In a future with even more advanced AI, a totalitarian government could effectively pre-empt and neutralize any opposition, freezing society in a permanent illiberal state that is difficult to reverse. For this reason, human rights defenders are pushing to codify prohibitions and limits before such systems become too pervasive. Even in democracies there is the danger of excessive use of AI in a harmful way: for example, in the future, the use of **predictive policing** (which combine ubiquitous monitoring and AI to anticipate crimes) could criminalize intentions or contexts rather than concrete acts, going against the principles of the rule of law. Not to mention the cyber risks: a malicious AI could design autonomously **cyberattacchi** sophisticated infrastructure, exponentially increasing the global cyber threat.

Towards man-machine coexistence: Many futurologists believe that we will progressively witness a growing fusion between biological and artificial intelligence. We already have it today **wearable and implantable devices** (intelligent pacemakers, brain neuroprostheses for Parkinson's, etc.). In the future, more refined brain-computer interfaces could directly connect our minds to AI systems, expanding our cognitive capabilities – a scenario hoped for by visionaries like Elon Musk (Neuralink project) to "keep pace" with advanced AI. This, however, opens up ethical dilemmas on personal identity, mental privacy (the **right to "neuroprivacy"** it will be crucial whether thoughts can be read or influenced by external AI). Furthermore, philosophical movements will probably emerge regarding the moral status of artificial intelligences themselves: if one day we will have machines capable of consciousness or at least complex human-like behavior, we will have to recognize in them some form of **right**? The concept of **rights of synthetic entities** appears science fiction today, but ethics and law scholars debate it from a long-term perspective, to avoid finding ourselves unprepared as we have been in the past when faced with sudden social revolutions.

Faced with these perspectives, there is a key element that will decide which path we will take: the **collective wisdom** with which we will face the advent of powerful AI. In other words, AI can be a **multiplier** both of our ingenuity and of our mistakes. If humanity is able to collaborate globally, put universal values first and govern technology in an inclusive way, then positive scenarios have a better chance of coming true. Conversely, if conflicts, political shortsightedness or the greed of a few prevail at the expense of the common good, AI could exacerbate existing problems or create new ones.

A note of caution was recently expressed by hundreds of experts and industry figures (including Elon Musk and some leading researchers) in a 2023 open letter calling for a **break of at least 6 months** in advanced AI projects, to reflect on security protocols, concerned by the uncontrolled pace at which increasingly powerful models (such as large language models such as GPT-4) are released
cam.ac.uk
. While not everyone agrees with the idea of a moratorium, the underlying

message is clear: **taking the time to understand and drive the technology** instead of being guided by it is fundamental.

Humanity's role in shaping its future: In conclusion, AI perhaps poses the fundamental question of what kind of future we want to build. It's not just a question of technology, but of **ethical and political vision**. AI forces humanity to look in the mirror: it amplifies our power, and with it our responsibility. If we continue on the path of human-centered development (*human-centered AI*), we will be able to leverage AI as an extension of our capabilities to build more just, prosperous and sustainable societies. Otherwise, we risk creating a world where technology gets out of hand or serves only narrow interests.

As Stephen Hawking effectively summarized: *"The rise of powerful AI will be either the best or worst thing to ever happen to humanity. We don't know which one yet."*
cam.ac.uk
. It is up to us to ensure, through wise choices in the present, that it is there **improve**. In the final chapter we will draw together what has been analysed, highlighting the main challenges and recommendations that have emerged in this journey between the past, present and future of technology and AI.

Conclusions

From the comparison between the technology of the 90s and today's technology, it is clear how profound the digital transformation of our society has been. In just a few decades we have moved from an analogue and localized world to a digital and globally interconnected one. THE'**information** has become instantaneous, the **communication** ubiquitous, and **production processes** automated and optimized by IT. The current revolution of**Artificial intelligence**, which represents both the natural continuation of that trend (thanks to computational power and big data) and a qualitative leap: for the first time we create systems capable of **learn** and make complex decisions almost like a human would.

The analysis carried out highlighted i **great benefits** already brought about by AI and potential future ones. AI can dramatically improve economic efficiency, create new wealth and free humanity from many burdensome jobs
weforum.org
. It can help us solve inextricable problems thanks to its ability to analyze data and find patterns beyond human possibilities. The prospects for positive application are practically limitless: healthcare, environment, education, transport, public services, entertainment, scientific research – wherever AI has something to offer in terms of optimization and innovation.

At the same time, we have explored the **critical issues and risks**. Without adequate countermeasures, AI could accentuate inequalities, replace many workers without offering them alternatives, violate privacy and rights if used for surveillance or discriminatory decisions, and even escape control and cause harm. We have seen how examples of algorithmic bias already exist today and how the international community is reacting with calls (UN, EU, etc.) to ban the most harmful uses
media.un.org

digital-strategy.ec.europa.eu
. Ethics provides us with compass and principles - fairness, transparency, accountability, human centrality - but their practical implementation requires concrete planning and governance efforts.

A common thread that emerged is the need to **rules and governance** effective. The European Union, with the AI Act, is blazing an important path, setting clear limits (bans on unacceptable practices such as social scoring and malicious manipulation) and compliance requirements for high-risk uses.

digital-strategy.ec.europa.eu

. This approach of *"responsible innovation"* it could become a model for others. At the same time, we need to invest in **culture and education**: Governments, companies and citizens must develop awareness of the potential and limits of AI, so that they can use and control it appropriately. Also promote the **AI safety research** and on "ethically aligned" AI is fundamental, to anticipate any future developments (such as AGI) with the necessary precautions.

An encouraging aspect is that these ethical and regulatory discussions have accompanied the technology since its inception more than ever. In the 1990s the Internet grew almost anarchically before society grasped its effects (positive and negative); for AI, we are seeing an earlier involvement of philosophers, jurists, citizens in the debate. This **multidisciplinary dialogue** is essential: AI is not just a question for engineers, but must be addressed with contributions from humanists, social scientists, economists, representatives of the social partners, minorities, etc., to build together a **shared vision** what AI do we want.

Ultimately, technological history teaches that humanity has been able to adapt and progress through every revolution - industrial, electrical, IT - facing enormous challenges but ultimately managing to improve its average living conditions. AI could amplify this virtuous trend if guided wisely. Or, in the absence of governance, it could generate painful discontinuities. It is up to us to direct the outcome. As the philosopher Huw Price, co-founder of the Center for the Future of Intelligence, said, *"The creation of artificial intelligence is probably a unique event in the history of the planet. It's a future we face together. Our goal is to build a community with a sense of common purpose to make this future the best it can be."*

cam.ac.uk

. This statement encapsulates the final message well: **a collective effort is needed** – from researchers to public and private stakeholders, up to individual citizens – to ensure that AI evolves as a positive force serving all humanity.

In conclusion, the journey from the technology of the 1990s to the AI of the present and future shows us a rapidly evolving landscape, full of promise but also complexity. We'll have to combine **innovation, prudence and humanism**. Innovation, to continue to push the limits of what is possible with AI, solving problems and creating opportunities. Prudence, to recognize risks and put in place rules and safeguards before it is late. Humanism, to constantly remind us that the well-being and dignity of man must be at the center of all technological progress. With this compass, we will be able to navigate the uncharted waters of the age of artificial intelligence, just as we have navigated those of the digital revolution, and arrive at a future where technology and humanity thrive together.

Bibliographical References:

- Fox, S. & Rainie, L. (2014). *Part 1: How the internet has woven itself into American life*. Pew Research Center – Internet & Technology. (Data on the use of PCs and the Internet in the USA in the 1980s and 1990s)
  pewresearch.org

  pewresearch.org
  .

- GWS Media (2021). *How System Requirements for Browsing the Internet Have Changed*. (Evolution of connection speeds: 14.4kbps modem in 1993, 56k dial-up in 1998)
  gwsmedia.com
  .

- Ritchie, H. et al. (2023). *Internet – Our World in Data*. (Global statistics: 63% of the population online by 2023, Internet user growth)
  ourworldindata.org
  .

- ANSA (2014). *The 90s and the digital revolution*. (Article reminiscent of the explosion of the Internet and mobile telephony in the 90s)
  ansa.it

  ansa.it

⬚ World Economic Forum / PwC (2017). *Report "Sizing the Prize"*. (St estimates economic impact of AI: +15.7 trillion $ by 2030, +14% global GDP)
weforum.org

weforum.org

⬚ McKinsey & Co. (2021). *Global Survey: State of AI*. (56% of companies have adopted AI in at least one function, increase compared to 2020)
mckinsey.com

⬚ Think Digital Partners / OECD (2018). *OECD now says 'only' 14% of jobs will be taken over by robots*. (OECD review: 14% jobs at high risk automation vs 47% estimated by Oxford)
thinkdigitalpartners.com

thinkdigitalpartners.com

⬚ Hicks, P. (OHCHR) (2021). *UN Press Conference on AI and Privacy*. (Bachelet, UN: request for moratorium on AI systems with high risk for rights, ban on applications incompatible with human rights)
media.un.org

media.un.org

⬚ European Commission, High-Level Expert Group on AI (2019). *Ethics Guidelines for Trustworthy AI*. (Seven requirements: human supervision, robustness and security, privacy, transparency, diversity/non-discrimination, social and environmental well-being, accountability)
digital-strategy.ec.europa.eu

digital-strategy.ec.europa.eu

digital-strategy.ec.europa.eu
.

⬚ European Commission (2021). *Proposal for an AI Act – Shaping Europe's Digital Future*. (EU AI Regulation: risk-based approach, bans on social scoring, manipulation and real-time biometrics; requirements for high-risk AI)
digital-strategy.ec.europa.eu
.

⬚ Hawking, S. (2016). *Launch speech of the Center for the Future of Intelligence, Univ. Cambridge*. (Quote: "The rise of powerful AI will be either the best or worst thing to ever happen to humanity. We don't know which yet.")
cam.ac.uk
.

⬚ Price, H. (2016). *Speech at the launch of the CFI*. (Quote: "The creation of artificial intelligence is probably a once in a lifetime event on the planet... our goal is to unite the community to make this future the best it can be.")
cam.ac.uk
.

Afterword

Throughout this essay we have explored the evolution of technology from the 1990s to today, analyzing the progress of artificial intelligence and its impact on contemporary society. We have journeyed through decades of innovation, moving from bulky computers and slow connections to pocket-sized devices with extraordinary potential, from rudimentary algorithms to advanced machine learning models capable of revolutionizing the way we live, work and interact with the world.

If there is one lesson that emerges strongly from this analysis, it is that technology is never an isolated phenomenon. Every advancement brings with it opportunities and risks, advantages and challenges. Artificial intelligence, in particular, presents itself as a very powerful tool, capable of improving the quality of life and accelerating human progress, but at the same time it raises crucial questions related to privacy, ethics and information control.

We find ourselves in a historical moment in which the regulation of AI and new technologies has become a central issue for governments, institutions and companies. The choices we make today will define the future, determining whether these innovations will be used equitably and sustainably or whether they will become tools of inequality and manipulation. Public awareness and debate are therefore fundamental for technological progress to be guided by principles of responsibility and inclusiveness.

But beyond the technical and political aspects, this journey through technology is also a human journey. Each innovation was born from the creativity, ingenuity and determination of men and women who imagined a different future and worked to make it real. It is to them, to the pioneers of the past and present, that we owe our ability to adapt and evolve in an increasingly digital world.

Looking to the future, we can only ask ourselves: what will be the next technological revolutions? What new challenges await us? The answer to these questions is uncertain, but one thing is clear: change is inevitable and, as always, it will be our use of technology that will determine whether this change will be a step forward for humanity or a danger to be faced.

With this essay, I wanted to offer food for thought on our relationship with technology, on the possibilities and responsibilities that it entails. The future is in our hands: it is up to us to choose how to shape it.

Index

Chapter 2 – Today's technology

2.1 The digital revolution and the power of modern hardware

- ⬚ Smartphones more powerful than old supercomputers, advanced chips, integrated artificial intelligence.
- ⬚ Ultra-fast connections and cloud computing.

2.2 Software, interfaces and new usage models

- ⬚ Modern operating systems, intuitive interfaces and cloud-based software.
- ⬚ Automation and artificial intelligence in data management.

2.3 Internet and global connectivity

- ⬚ The spread of 5G, always active connections and instant access to information.
- ⬚ The impact of connectivity on work, education and socialization.

Chapter 3 – Technological evolution: from 1990 to today

3.1 From personal computing to the mobile era

- ⬚ The evolution from desktop computers to multifunction smartphones.
- ⬚ Miniaturization, increase in computing power and democratization of technology.

3.2 The web revolution and the digital economy

- ⬚ From e-commerce to social networks: the internet as the hub of economic and social interactions.
- ⬚ The shift from static sites to user-generated content.

3.3 Artificial intelligence as a new paradigm

- From early chatbot experiments to modern machine learning systems.
- The integration of AI into daily life and production processes.

Chapter 4 – The advancement of Artificial Intelligence

4.1 From early models to advanced systems

- Evolution of AI from the 1990s to today: from expert systems to deep learning.
- Advances in neural networks and the development of machine learning.

4.2 Le milestone dell'IA: Deep Blue, Watson, AlphaGo

- Key historical moments that marked the rise of artificial intelligence.
- Specialized AI vs. General AI: limits and opportunities.

4.3 Generative artificial intelligence and the future of automation

- From text and image creation to conversational AI (ChatGPT, DALL-E).
- Implications for creativity, misinformation, and ethical use.

Chapter 5 – AI in everyday life

5.1 Smartphones, voice assistants and home automation

- How AI has transformed our relationship with electronic devices.

5.2 AI in social media, search and streaming

☐ Recommendation algorithms and their impact on our choices and behaviors.

5.3 Banks, healthcare and finance: AI in essential services

☐ Optimization of financial operations, assisted medical diagnoses, fraud prevention.

Chapter 6 – Artificial Intelligence and Economy

6.1 The impact of AI on global productivity

☐ Automation of business processes and economic growth.

6.2 Inequalities and redistribution of wealth

☐ AI as a driver of innovation, but also a possible amplifier of economic gaps.

6.3 The role of technology companies and regulations

☐ The rise of tech giants and the need for regulations for a fair market.

Chapter 7 – Artificial Intelligence and Work

7.1 Automation and replacement of professions

☐ Which jobs are at risk and what new roles will be created by AI.

7.2 The risk of polarization of the labor market

⬚ Technological unemployment and the need for professional retraining.

7.3 Strategies for an AI at the service of workers

⬚ Training, protection policies and new working models.

Chapter 8 – Artificial Intelligence and Privacy

8.1 The massive collection of personal data

⬚ The problem of profiling, digital tracking and surveillance.

8.2 Information security in the age of AI

⬚ Risks of hacking, data manipulation and improper use of sensitive information.

8.3 Regulatory and technological solutions for privacy

⬚ GDPR, strong encryption and data protection regulations.

Chapter 9 – Artificial Intelligence and Human Rights

9.1 Freedom of expression and AI

⬚ Algorithmic filters, automated censorship and the risk of information bubbles.

9.2 Discrimination and bias in AI models

⬚ The problem of algorithms that reproduce and amplify

stereotypes and prejudices.

9.3 AI in security and justice

⬜ The risk of autonomous weapons and the use of AI in mass surveillance.

Chapter 10 – AI in the future of humanity: prospects and challenges

10.1 Positive scenarios: an AI-enhanced world

⬜ How artificial intelligence could improve human life in many sectors.

10.2 Dystopian scenarios and future risks

⬜ The danger of total control and a hyper-surveillance society.

10.3 AI governance and global regulation

⬜ The need for international collaboration to drive AI development.

Conclusion

⬜ **Summary of the analysis carried out:** Technological progress and the impact of AI.

⬜ **Human responsibility:** How we can drive technological development in an ethical and sustainable way.

⬜ **Questions for the future:** What will be the next big change and how can we prepare?